Psychological Nutrition

Psychological Nutrition

Shoba Sreenivasan Ph.D.
Linda E Weinberger Ph.D.

HOLYMOLYPRESS

For more information visit www.holymolypress.com

Copyright @ 2015 Shoba Sreenivasan Ph.D./Linda E Weinberger Ph.D.
Cover design by May Abdellatif

ISBN-10: 0985360496
ISBN-13: 9780985360498

TABLE OF CONTENTS

INTRODUCTION

Psychological Nutrition is not a concept that most women have ever really contemplated. We don't consider our emotions and reactions within the context of nourishment. Consequently, we unthinkingly consume a diet of negative emotions and thereby allow no room for positive emotions. This mindset is particularly true for those of us who are in middle-age or older and who have that "hyper-responsible" gene. The concepts that we introduce– emotional anorexia, binge emotions, emotional jelly belly, and psychological malnourishment-will ring an intuitive bell.

Psychological malnutrition has a profoundly harmful effect. It keeps us in the same emotionally unsatisfying loop– one that is fed by a false sense of obligation. It keeps us unsatisfied with our lives, our work, and our relationships; it keeps us closing doors to opportunities. Ultimately, it can destroy our marriages, our friendships, and our family relationships through martyrdom, insincere niceness, and doing for others with resentment rather than love.

All of this ultimately is what keeps the arteries of our soul clogged with "high fat" emotions.

As you glance at the Chapters listed, you'll see that the purpose of this book is not toward achieving giddy happiness (although we want you to have that). Rather, our purpose is to encourage you to become incredibly creative and energized. We want to inspire you to unleash your full potential, and to fulfill your passion and destiny. While that sounds very exciting and positive, the truth is, you won't be able to do it if you're in a psychologically malnourished state.

This book will explain how people, and in particular women, can achieve and maintain Psychological Nutrition. Our interactions with people, as well as our reactions to events, can have a profound effect on our mental health. The Chapters in the book discuss the numerous situations we find ourselves in when we experience "high-cost emotions," how and why we react as we do, and ways in which we can take control and attain positive mental health.

The authors happen to be clinical psychologists; but more importantly, we are women in some stage of middle age who discovered that we are at a turning point in our lives. We're no different than millions of other people—women and men, young and old—who want to live a physically and mentally healthier and more enriched life. How you go about doing that is the basis of this book. And what you achieve—for yourself and for those with whom you share your bounty—is the ultimate aim.

CHAPTER 1

Psychological Nutrition: High-Cost Emotions and Emotional Calories

Tina had counted calories for as long as she could remember which at 50 was a good bit of time. And she had cheated on the calorie count for about the same stretch. Now she was in dangerous territory: the bakery section of the grocery store where she was considering a small Bundt cake.

Brushed with Belgian chocolate and sprinkled with toffee for a truly delightful afternoon treat.

Hmmm. She turned it over to read the nutritional label for due diligence: it said, "150 calories a serving." Only 150 calories a serving! Yes, she believed it—all this took was ignoring that there was a total of 10 servings in one Bundt cake. Her eyes twitched. Her mouth felt dry. A sour taste coated her tongue.

She felt completely burned out from the day. Tina looked at the cake again: one serving meant an itty bitty slice. Well, she would just stick to one serving. Didn't she deserve a treat? Yes, indeed she did. Hadn't her best client left her today for another firm? Didn't her boss just give her office to the young and cute new hire whom he was "mentoring" and moved Tina into the broom closet (not literally, but pretty damn close)? She desperately needed a delightful treat. But, could she stick to one serving? Who was she kidding? That "serving" was so small that it wouldn't satisfy the chocolate cravings of an ant. Oh, who cared! Tina threw the cake into her shopping cart.

Now, what is interesting is that after eating that cake (yes, all of it in one fell swoop) Tina did not feel better. It had, as you might astutely guess, the opposite effect. Now she felt bloated, angry, irritated, upset with herself, *and* burned out.

Wait. Wait. Before you throw down this book in disgust thinking, "Yeah, I know all about stress eating, binge eating, emotional eating, impulse buying, and all the remedies: make a list before you grocery shop, don't shop for food when you're hungry, or tired, or blah, blah, blah. I don't need another book to tell me that. Plus, isn't it true that some foods do relieve emotional distress–if not, missy experts, why are they called 'comfort foods?'" What was Tina supposed to do? Stuff her face with a bag of raw kale?

No arguments there. We'd go for the cake over kale too. Judge not lest ye be judged. Who hasn't been Tina?

But, this isn't a book about dieting. At least not the way you might think– no one is going to stop you (or Tina) from eating that cake.

In fact, this book isn't about food at all. It's not about sustenance in the physical realm.

Psychological Nutrition

This is a book about psychological nourishment. Feelings are the ingredients. Relationships and events are the products you consume. Emotional reactions are the calories they cost. And just as with food, some bloat you, weigh you down, and add baggage around the middle, while others energize and nourish you.

Recall what drove Tina to eat the whole cake anyway: she was feeling burned out. Burned. Out. Think of a fireplace with logs; before the fire is set, the logs are whole and sturdy. Then the fire is set, and slowly the flames begin to form small licks at first, then they are raging. Soon you can't even see the logs anymore. Quickly the logs are devoured, and the flames die down to nothing. Now all that's left are ashes where the logs once were. They are burned out. That's the analog to emotions: if you begin the day with logs and end up with ashes, you are burned out. What made Tina feel burned out? Her boss and the crappy day, you say (and think); isn't that obvious?

Hmm. Maybe. But how do you know that? How much emotional energy did she start the day with? How did that power get used up? Maybe she was running on empty for a long time. Is it possible that she was "burned out" long before the day started?

Is it possible that the bad breaks happened because she was already emotionally spent? Maybe that led to the client leaving; maybe it led to sloppiness and negativity that caused her boss to decide to mentor someone more enthusiastic? Most likely, it was more than just that one bad day.

Psychological nutrition comes from feelings which the ingredients.

Let's step back and consider this: just as your body requires a certain amount of caloric energy to run smoothly, so too does your psyche require a certain amount of emotional energy to function. While flour, sugar, baking powder, butter, salt, chocolate, and eggs make up the cake, so too do emotions make up the elements of your day-day-to day experiences.

This is the core concept, which is worth repeating: Whether you are psychologically nourished or malnourished is contingent upon the "food" you put into your psyche. That food is your feelings– how you react, how you interpret, how you view the world. The food that you consume; that is, the products, come in these two broad packages: relationships and events. How you interpret and emotionally respond to the relationships and events are *the calories they cost.*

Adverse events and reactions are high-fat, high cost, and low benefit; they deplete the amount of psychological energy you have. Positive developments and reactions are low-fat and high benefit; they add to the psychological energy you have. And just like with food, some relationships and events are toxic--you may have allergic reactions to them, they constipate or burden you--while other experiences energize and nourish you and allow you to move to new heights. Just like electricity, this psychological energy can be generated or depleted.

How? It's a simple formula. Emotions that increase or produce energy are nourishing. Those that consume energy are unhealthy or toxic. Our day is made up of units of experiences; there are those that add energy value, those that take away, and some that are just neutral (We'll discuss these later). Feelings are the primary unit that make up the ingredients of a psychological experience. No big news here, right? But, think about Tina again; she was burned out– meaning that she was running in negative energy numbers. She had moved into and used up her reserve.

How did this happen? If we know that feelings or emotional reactions are related to what we experience during the day, why do we engage in those that make us feel depleted? High-cost emotions are high caloric items–they are empty emotions that weigh you down and deplete your psychological reserves. Just like high fat, high-calorie foods don't nourish but add cholesterol deposits, fat around the belly, etc., high-cost emotions add fat around your emotional belly (and we'll tell you how they also add to your physical belly). Yes, you say, "I got it." There are umpteen books and motivational speakers out there who tell us, "stay positive, release endorphins, increase serotonin neurotransmitters with your attitude!"

Relationships and events are the products you consume.

Yes, yes, you say. "Got it. I know all this." Still, "got it" and "doing it" don't always go together.

Why do most of us do this anyway–run the same race of doing too much, being overburdened, and then like Tina, feeling burned out? It's not that we're stupid: this pattern is evident even in women who hold multiple advanced degrees, have the veneer of success, and are doing it all.

If we know all this, why do we continually expend emotional energy down into the negative numbers? Why do any of us do this over and over (and we all do) until it just drains us dry? It just doesn't make sense. Ugh.

Emotional reactions are the calories they cost.

We suggest this explanation culled from our long experience, both personally as well as professionally as mental health clinicians: we do this because we have no clue, much less awareness, as to when, where, why, and how we are using up psychological energy.

In fact, we aren't even aware of the state of our emotional tank (on full, half-full, or empty) because this is something that we are not trained to assess. Physical needs for food are easily detected—a growling stomach, headache from low blood sugar—but, emotional needs for nourishment are much less obvious. But, okay, how do you become aware? We'll tell you in a minute.

First, let's go back to Tina. Recall, when she was in the grocery store looking at the nutritional content of the cake. It was right there for her to see and assess. But, you might argue, so what? Didn't Tina choose to buy the cake anyway? Didn't she elect to eat the whole thing, even knowing the nutritional content? Yes. We're not saying having information always leads to good decision-making, but knowledge is nonetheless power. It tells you about the terrain of the land you are traversing. You can decide to eat the cake, but now you know that this was 1,500 calories you spent on that item; maybe it changes your behavior, maybe it doesn't. But, if you had no awareness that the cake was 1,500 calories and consumed it as well as many other high caloric items, what would be the result–morbid obesity, most likely. Knowledge gives you choice. And this book and our concepts are ultimately about that: a way to promote making educated decisions. Later on, you will see the value of doing so. Right now, let's just go over the basic concepts so that you can test-run it in your life.

> **The food that you consume; that is, the products, come in these two broad packages: relationships and events.**

Pick up a product you've bought at the grocery store. Let's say a box of macaroni and cheese. What's the first thing you see?

The name of the product: "Cheesy Mac-N-Cheese."

The next thing is the description: "a whole grain take on a classic favorite: velvety smooth, mild cheddar cheese smothering whole wheat rosemary infused penne."

Flip the box and you will see some more descriptions of the product: "A smooth buttery treat for those who crave this classic comfort food. Made from a blend of three cheeses to maximize flavor, but with subtle hints of cinnamon, fennel and allspice, this mac-n-cheese will tantalize and satisfy." This narrative is designed to sell you on the product, to tempt your taste-buds.

Next comes a listing of the nutritional value and the FDA example for macaroni and cheese.

No pretty words, just the FDA facts to allow you to make an informed decision. There is also another piece of interesting information listed: expiration dates. A product to be consumed does not last forever; you should use it by a given date.

Otherwise, it may have an unfavorable taste, cause health problems, or have less nutritional value than initially identified.

> **How you interpret and emotionally respond to the relationships and events are the calories they cost.**

Psychological Nutrition Labels

Now, imagine if the events that you are going to confront during your day had a psychological nutritional label.

Let's use this example. Your family–meaning your adult brother and sister–have decided that it is important for the whole family to spend Thanksgiving week with your elderly parents in the state where they live.

The event is going to be a double celebration. Your oldest sibling is getting remarried, and your parents are also celebrating their 60th wedding anniversary.

The entire family has not been together for at least a decade. It may look like this:

Front Box: Quality Time with Family

Back Box: Truly a Thanksgiving!

Small print details: You have to travel 2,000 miles; your sister and brother reside near your parents who now live in a senior residence community.

Your sister insists that you stay in her home so as to "bond again" and to "have "sleepover fun." Therefore, you cannot get a hotel room because this would be highly insulting.

You will be sleeping on a sofa-bed in your sister's house.

Your husband refuses; he will go to a hotel.

Your sister's husband is a know-it-all, big mouth who insists on ruining every event with charged political discussion.

Because your brother has a cat, and your Aunt May is allergic to dander, Thanksgiving is at your sister's house.

Your brother is marrying a "bimbo" 20 years younger than he who is clearly after his money.

This is your sister's opinion which she stated to you over the phone (as said "bimbo" has insulted your sister by telling her she will not be a bridesmaid).

Your adult daughter cannot attend due to her job demands–your parents are upset.

Your brother's children are not attending because they hate the bimbo. Your parents want you to be the peacemaker.

Look at the barebones psychological nutritional facts.

PSYCHOLOGICAL NUTRITION FACTS
SERVINGS: 7 DAYS
AMOUNT: 1
EMOTIONAL CONTENT
    HIGH FAT EMOTIONS: 90%: IRRITATION, ANGER, GUILT, RESENTMENT
    LOW FAT EMOTIONS: 10% AFFECTION
WARNING: CONSUMPTION OF THIS PRODUCT WILL BE HAZARDOUS TO YOUR EMOTIONAL HEALTH.

Ask yourself this: If you had this label for the event, would you attend?

In fact, the answer is likely, "no," you wouldn't–at least, not the way it is packaged. But our experiences and obligations do not come with psychological nutrition labels. In fact, it is likely that you would attend, or are planning to, or have attended similar family situations that are as pleasant as nails driven through your eyeballs.

Why?

Because many of us, and women in particular, plunge headlong into peril just like the scenario above because we feel the pressure of obligations: to family, employers, and friends. And out of guilt, a desire to be helpful, to be a pleaser, to be everything to everyone everywhere and forevermore.

Of course, no one can do this. In fact, one shouldn't do it because it is counterproductive to healthy functioning. In short, we ignore the warnings and end up in the bakery section like Tina looking to a Bundt cake for solace.

Okay, you say. That's interesting: a nutrition label for obligations that we encounter. But come on, no one "prints out" psychological nutrition labels.

True, but wouldn't it be interesting if they did? What would it tell you about the decisions that you make? How would it influence you? Making psychological nutrition labels is exactly what we will encourage YOU to do.

To begin the process you need some basic concepts and we will provide you with a method of self-assessment. Whoa--don't throw the book down, this isn't difficult; we're not adding another obligation; we won't have you writing endless useless information in a workbook. Believe us you can do this-we did and we're just as busy and prone to being everywoman as you.

Overview of psychological nutrition: We are all familiar (too familiar, you might say) with calories in a nutritional context. Calories are units of energy. You put units of energy into your body (by consuming food) as well as take them out (by exercising, your daily activities). Excess units (calories) are unneeded energy that get turned into body fat. This storage is, purportedly, for later use; but really it just sort of hangs on our bodies collecting in the most unflattering places. That's food.

Bad food– empty calories–are products that don't nourish the body but wear and break it down (like high-fat foods that deposit cholesterol, or high sugar products that impact on the functioning of your kidneys, liver, heart etc.) and the body breaks down (heart attack, cancer, liver failure, diabetes, etc.).

Now, emotions are also units of energy. By analogy, in psychological nutrition, negative emotions are like those empty calories that deplete the body. Negative emotions don't add energy; they break down psychological stamina. Positive emotions, however, augment psychological reserves.

So, the basic concept is this: Empty emotional calories are negative emotions that you put into yourself, and ones that will eventually burn you out. They cause psychological starvation; it's as if you were eating paper or a non-nourishing substance. These are what we call high-fat emotions.

Women plunge headlong into peril because we feel the pressure of obligations to family, employers, and friends; a desire to be helpful, to be a pleaser, to be everything to everyone, everywhere, and forevermore.

Concept 1 High-fat emotions: These are emotions that you impulsively engage in that are negative, energy draining, and bad for you (junk emotions, like junk food): they create psychological pain and can heighten the perception of physical pain as well. They require no discipline, just knee-jerk emotional reactivity. They are downhill walking (and tripping) and require no development of emotional muscles. They form an emotional jelly-belly.

Examples: guilt, resentment, anger, bitterness, jealousy, depression, anxiety, worry, feeling less-than, fear, doubt and second-guessing yourself, hurried/agitated internal state, pessimism, frustration, conflictual/adversarial impulses. These are all junk emotions like junk food. A diet of these emotions is unhealthy.

Concept 2 Low-fat emotions: These are emotions that you have to work at keeping in the forefront of your psychological functioning and ones that you should promote. They are positive, energy augmenting, and good for you. They require practice, because they are "uphill" walking, are not impulsive, and require emotional muscle building and discipline (but surprisingly not a lot--believe us we did this and it hasn't been difficult).

Examples: excitement, enthusiasm, optimism, calmness, contentment, joy, focused attention, clear thinking, laser-like concentration, creative impulses, fun-oriented, humor seeking, cooperative and collaborative impulses.

Concept 3 High-fat emotions drain; Low-fat emotions energize

Negative emotions are exhausting. They drain you. You know that. They suck creativity and fun out of your life; they poison your inner self and close doors to opportunity.

Positive emotions do the opposite; they energize you and open up your world, both in terms of your inner self and the doors to opportunity.

Concept 4 Psychological energy is a resource that can be depleted or increased.

You begin each day with a certain amount of psychological energy. The amount may be in the negative numbers or the positive numbers. Just like your bank account–you have a certain sum of money; if you continue to spend while not replenishing, you will eventually end up in the negative numbers (or the analog: in emotional bankruptcy).

The amount of psychological energy that you have available is dependent on you and how you decide to organize your emotional life. You may have spent a lifetime drawing out without putting in, and therefore, like Tina in our example, you are running on empty. Eventually, whether it's a vehicle or a person, an entirely empty tank won't allow a car to run or a person to function without causing damage to oneself.

Concept 5 Emotional pyramids. Just like the food pyramid, there are emotional pyramids. You can find them in psychological theory (such as Abraham Maslow's hierarchy of needs), and we provide reference materials for those who are interested in further study.

Here's a typical way to construct that pyramid, following standard psychological theory, as applied to psychological nutrition.

The base of the pyramid consists of the emotions that run your everyday life: basic attentiveness, orientation to remaining alert and aware.

The next level up in the pyramid are emotions that are social lubricants; these help avoid conflict; such as, biting your tongue, engaging in social niceties.

The level above is the need for affiliation. Humans are group animals; we like to feel like we belong somewhere. These are the emotions you need to keep intimate relationships going, work going, friendships going.

The next set of emotional needs have to do with your sense of self: this is the running commentary many of us engage in, mostly doing so unconsciously; these are our reactions and how it impacts on the view we have of ourselves.

The last, smallest and uppermost cap of the pyramid is your inner core sense of destiny. After you get all of the basic stuff done–your ability to function day-to-day, the go-along-to-get-along, the people- pleasing so that you're not an outcast, and the sense of yourself–then you can focus on the luxury item of your inner self-actualization. Now, this makes sense, doesn't it?

No, it does not! Let's repeat that. No, it does not!

Flip that pyramid content! We want the cap- that drive to fulfill your creative self- to be where you are focused at all times. That should be the base, the solid foundation of who you are and what drives you.

We want you to consider this: you can have size 20 feet (the standard survival base, or the bottom of the pyramid) but if your heart isn't beating (the pyramid tip), you won't be standing. Look at how the pyramid is typically constructed for psychological hierarchies; most of one's time is spent in fundamental survival mode, next is the social functioning, and then the self-esteem stuff, and last, at the tippy top are the drives to get you to inner satisfaction.

Negative emotions clog your creative arteries, they kill inspiration.

Why do we assume that this inner satisfaction is a luxury item-something that you save for and get (if ever) sometime in the far away future?

Because the narrative of the lowest common denominator–that of basic survival– requires very little or no effort. Many of us have been trained to think that reaching for more, especially that tip of the pyramid, is reserved only for the special few. We believe that the tip of the pyramid is out of reach for us common-folk, the everyday woman living in obscurity, and that the tip is unrealistic, idealistic, and perhaps even foolish. No, best to stay with what you know, do the same-old, same-old, the safe and tried and true route. It's called survival.

Remember, Bundt cake gobbling is survival mode living.

Alert. We're not selling survival: we're promoting potential. This entire book is geared towards that: to break out of emotional narratives that keep you locked out of achieving your destiny and walking with your head down, hunched over, feeding the emotional jelly-belly. Being helpful Helen, Pity-party Penelope, Sad-faced Sally, Angry Angie, you get it. Anything that has kept you from getting what you want and being your best and most fulfilled self is something that has to go. Throw it out of your emotional closet. It is outdated on you. That was the learning curve when you were young and didn't know any better. Now you are a grown-up woman, and this is an adult philosophy. We want you to be full of elegance, sophistication, and confidence. Don't be deterred by these big statements. Fulfilling the best in ourselves and not bottom-dwelling in survival mode is where we should all be living. You'll see why as these chapters progress.

Taking an Emotional Inventory. An inventory means taking stock of what you have. A well-known psychological inventory, the "Minnesota Multiphasic Inventory" has 567 questions geared toward tapping into psychological traits and approaches.

This is NOT what we mean by an emotional inventory. You will be engaging in psychological self-assessment, but nothing complicated. This is taking stock of your emotional life. It does not have to be on an hour-to-hour, day-to-day basis for the rest of your life. It just a method for you to begin living in an emotionally mindful manner.

Positive emotions open up the imagination and opportunities.

Stop. Don't sigh and say I don't have time for all that (WE did and had to readjust our thinking. We're only giving you what we experienced with this). You do have the time. This effort will be a very simple, painless exercise- well, not painless because self-assessment will illuminate what you may have been trying to cloak in darkness.

But, let's cut to the chase.

7-day Snapshot. Stop. No, not a workbook (we promised, remember?) This is all you will have to do:

1. Go to a drugstore or big-box store and buy a small notebook that you can slip in your purse (cost should be about $1.95 to $3.95).

2. Buy a pen that you can clip onto it.
3. For seven days starting right when you wake up record the following: emotion, trigger, and value

Don't engage in judgment, don't try to change anything. Just rate it (no neutral ratings for this exercise).

This exercise is an assessment, a self-learning. It is analogous to a pre-diet inventory of what types of food you consume and their caloric value.

Emotional Inventory Date: June 21
Emotion: rested, content (6:21 am.)
Trigger: sunshine through window
Value: +/energized

Emotion: distracted/agitated (7:40 am.)
Trigger: multi-tasking, hurrying
Value: -/depleting

Emotion: irritated (8:00 a.m.)
Trigger: interrupted by chatty co-worker
Value: -/depleting

Emotion: anxious (8:32 am.)
Trigger: picked up voicemail that plumber won't make it to fix clogged bathroom
Value: -/depleting

At the end of the 7-day period go back and calculate for each day the values; i.e., the number of negatives and positives and then the total. This diary will give you an idea for each day of whether you had gained emotional energy or were in the depleted range.

7-Day Calculation Tally

	Postive	Negative
Day 1		
Day 2		
Day 3		
Day 4		
Day 5		
Day 6		
Day 7		

Calculate the same for the week. Now you will know where you stand in terms of how you use emotional energy. It will explain why you either feel sluggish/burned out or energized. It will give you a snapshot view of whether you are psychologically nourished or malnourished. Later, we give you a way to construct a much more detailed assessment. But start with this. The 7-day snapshot will point to the people, places, events, reactions that either lift you up or bring you down.

This 7-day snapshot will be a useful guide for understanding the psychological nutritional content of events and how to develop labels for experiences that have occurred.

It will also form the base for developing labels for events or experiences that are upcoming. Knowing the ratio of your daily negative to positive emotional energy gives you something very powerful: knowledge. That knowledge says you have a choice, because who controls your reactions but you?

This process will then allow you to make your own psychological nutrition labels for your daily products (that is, the events, the interactions, the relationships you have in your life).

PSYCHOLOGICAL NUTRITION FACTS
SERVINGS:
AMOUNT:
EMOTIONAL CONTENT
HIGH FAT EMOTIONS:
LOW FAT EMOTIONS:
WARNING:

Assess it. We want you to get in the habit of assessing the psychological nutritional content of the commitments that you have made to, people and events that come across your path, or opportunities or invitations. Assess it. You will find that some things are just too costly because they are hazardous to your emotional health. You will have to cut out these events/people/places in order to grow your creative core.

Negative emotions clog your creative arteries, they kill inspiration.

Remember, Bundt cake gobbling is survival mode living.

Positive emotions open up the imagination and opportunities. They move you away from a tunnel vision perspective, or one where you have your head down in a hunched posture. They move you to standing upright with your eyes lifted high to the mountain that you will conquer.

CHAPTER 2

Expiration Dates: Tossing Spoiled Emotional Products from the Psychological Pantry

Assessing the psychological nutritional content of your life requires assigning expiration dates. Some reactions are toxic because you are consuming a "spoiled" emotional product. Some obligations and relationships are, likewise, past their use-by date.

Let's look at food products as an analogy. Food products have an interesting informational element: expiration dates. Why? Because we want to know the quality of a food: is it still healthy to consume? For example, some foods have a long "shelf life," where they remain nutritious and taste good. Other foods spoil quickly and have a very short "shelf-life." With time, however, almost all foods lose their full nutritional value and the quality of their taste (for example, turning rancid).

Just like some foods decay in a short period of time, while others may take years- so do relationships. Relationships just like food—have an expiration date.

Psychological Nutrition

Think about it for awhile. Have you ever known a person with whom you once had a good relationship but as time went on that relationship changed? Maybe it grew stale, or maybe it became harmful for you—dangerous to your emotional health. What did you do? Did you end it or did you let it go on but with increasingly less contact such that it died a natural death? Or did you go on as always and accept it? Or did you continue the relationship but with the hope that it might change one day? Or did you wait for the other person to act?

Frequently we are told this: There is no right or wrong response; it all depends on you and what you believe is best, given everything.

Well. Not really.

That's a polite way of reframing that sometimes the season of the relationship is over. The problem is that women are oriented toward niceness. Nice girl. Good girl. Obedient girl. Placating girl. We use the term girl because maturity belongs to the title "woman." These are junior high girl reactions. You are a fully grown woman. Junior high clothes on you would look terrible. Junior high emotions are just about as flattering.

It's important to recognize that sometimes a friendship sours or it goes flat. Also, remember the type and amount of psychological energy you have is dependent on what your emotional diet. If most of your relationships are stale, sour, or poisonous, your psychological reserves will be in the negative. Consequently, you will feel sluggish, flat, bitter, defeated. No new ideas, exciting opportunities or events are likely to come your way. And if they do, you will be so mired in the negative emotional force field that you will repel them. It is important to really look at this, to understand the landscape of your psychological life, to know what you are consuming psychologically each day.

Before you assess what "spoiled" emotional products are in your psychological pantry, you need to get a detailed sense of your emotional nutritional landscape. We began in Chapter 1, with a discussion of psychological nutrition using Tina as an example. In fact, for most of us, an issue that has received a great deal of attention in recent years is our interest in the foods we consume. We are becoming more aware and inquisitive about food, and like Tina we look to the nutrition content to be conscious of the product. What's in it? How many calories does it have? What is its sodium content? How many preservatives and artificial ingredients does it have? Many companies advertise this information, believing that the consumer wants to know and will buy a particular product if it's low in sodium, "lite," gluten-free, organic, etc. Some of us are so concerned about these issues that we're willing to pay more for the product if we believe that it is healthy for us.

This awareness of the nutritional composition of our foods can be viewed as a positive approach to taking care of our body. "Continue to eat food that is good for you; try and eliminate, or at a minimum, cut back on the 'not so healthy' food even though it tastes delicious." Many of us will do all these things because we want to be healthy; we want to live longer; we want to avoid or control physical ailments. We may even do this because of other influences—to fit in with a circle of people, to be in better shape for our job, to heed the advice of those who care about us, or to look more attractive. But we all know if you aren't motivated to eat well and take care of your body, all the pressure, threats, cajoling, and subtle (or not so subtle) hints won't work or be maintained in the long run.

That which we consume, medically speaking, is fuel for the body. What we choose to put in our bodies has a significant impact on our physical health. Our increasing desire to know more about what we're eating and our assessment of whether "it's good for us" is a positive direction to take for achieving and maintaining our physical health. That which we psychologically consume- our reactions to others, the relationships, the decisions we make- these fuel our psyche. Similarly, what emotions we put in our psyches has a significant impact on our psychological health.

In the first chapter, we asked the question: what about out psychological health? What do we do to keep ourselves emotionally healthy? Do we approach our mental health in any way close to the way we do our physical health? Do we actually examine and evaluate what makes us FEEL good or what makes us feel BAD, or whatever it is we FEEL? Probably not. We concluded that we do not assess psychological nutrition.

Situational circumstances and people tend to be the primary precipitants of emotional reactions for most of us. How are you feeling now, this minute, this hour, this day, this week, etc.? Who made you feel that way? What made you feel that way? These are the elements that constitute the ingredients of emotional "products."

What we propose is that you develop psychological nutritional labels for your life. That is, that you think seriously about and commit to improving your ratio of high-fat (negative) to low-fat (positive) emotions. In other words, pay attention to your emotional health. To do this, you will have to undergo a check-up to determine the extent of your emotional responses. That is, looking at the emotions you experience, do they fall in the positive or healthy range? Are there healthy emotions that you do not experience at all (the good low-fat kind); such as happiness, love, and appreciation? In order to construct informative psychological nutritional labels you have to understand of the terrain of your emotional day.

How do you do it? In the first chapter, we suggested that you buy a small notebook to give you a very brief psychological nutritional overview-the 7-day Snap-shot. It was an approach that was very similar to assessing the nutritional value of foods. This chapter will go into more detail, give an example of a diary, and conclude with the idea of expiration dates- how some relationships, events, and feelings that you engage in are long expired products.

But first, let's look at how to construct an emotional inventory/ diary. This is a process toward mindful emotional living. The reward is being freed of the innumerable emotions are draining. It means opening up that psychological pantry and cleaning it out and tossing out spoiled emotional products. How?

Let's go back to the food analogy. Maybe some of you have tried a diet plan where you record all that you eat and assign a score to each particular food item, so as to let you know what type and how much food you can eat in a day. You chart and evaluate what you eat as soon as you eat it. You don't wait later to register your score because you may unknowingly exceed your limit and defeat the purpose of losing weight and getting or staying healthy. Then you forget to chart, because it is just way too complicated. Or, you chart inconsistently. We're not going there. We actually want you to be able to do an emotional inventory!

Therefore, we suggest a simpler method. Remember, it's toward promoting emotional health and engaging in good psychological nutrition. Also, ultimately all of this is geared toward unleashing your creativity, a process that cannot happen if you are "all gunked up" with high-fat emotions.

Okay. So, yes this "emotional diary" is similar to the "food diary" in that it does require a bit of time commitment (not a lot, but you do need to write down emotions, triggers, and their value), a genuine assessment of your feelings, and an awareness of what precipitated that emotion.

Constructing the Psychological Nutrition Label.

Of course you won't have a nutritional label already printed to guide you. You're the one who will have to assign a value to the person or situation. You are the FDA and will have to print your label.

How? The approach has you examine your relationships (people) and events to assess if they are negative or "high-fat" (similar to high in calories, high in saturated fat, high in sodium—in other words, not so good for you) or positive or low-fat (low in calories, high in fiber, high in calcium, high in protein—in other words, they are good for your health). We are only interested in recording those emotions that have a positive or negative value; neutral reactions to events or people are not recorded because they neither help nor harm your emotional state.

Remember, this is an assessment as to the emotional (nutritional) content of your interactions with people and reactions to events. In order to "toss" spoiled products, you have to know what you are consuming on a day to day basis. As we said, in many ways, it's similar to keeping any type of diary, except here you record information regarding the events/feelings and note your reactions close to when they occur. You **don't** have to be obsessive about it. However, once you get a sense of the "valence" of your reactions, that is are they positive or negative, that will allow you to construct the psychological nutrition label. Let's start with the rating system and move through an example to illustrate the approach.

The Rating System:

Low fat (positive emotions) are rated a +

High fat (negative emotions) are rated a –

You can also assign one or two plusses or minuses to indicate the degree of a positive or negative emotional reaction, if you wish to have a better idea of the degree of low or high fact emotions you experienced during the charted period.

STEP 1: BUY THE NOTEBOOK AND A SMALL PEN

STEP 2: WRITE THESE THREE THINGS IN THE NOTEBOOK

Date Time	Trigger	Emotion	Value	(+/-)

Example

Date: September 18

Time	Trigger	Emotion	Value	(+/-)
8:00 am	stuck in traffic	frustrated	-	
8:30 am	song on radio	energized	+	

STEP 3: POP THE NOTEBOOK IN YOUR PURSE AND WRITE DOWN THE EMOTIONS/TRIGGERS DURING THE DAY

Just carry the small notebook that you can pop in your purse and jot briefly the emotion, trigger, and value (+/-). See, it's not difficult at all.

STEP 4: ASSESSMENT

At the end of a week you would calculate the number of positive (low fat) emotions and the number of negative (high fat) emotions. You could even look at the ratio of how many were in the double (e.g., ++ or –) symbols. If you are mathematically inclined, you can analyze your reactions even further by calculating the percentages of each type of positive and negative emotion. For example, if on Day 1 you had a total of 20 emotions, 10 of which were low fat positive emotions and 10 being high fat negative emotions, that's a simple calculation indicating a 50% +, 50%- distribution. In Chapter 1 we introduced the concept of a 7-day calculation tally.

This 7-day snapshot will give you an idea of the peaks and valleys of your emotional terrain. The process of an emotional inventory does require being highly attuned to your feelings and willingness to be honest about how you feel and why. No one has to see this but you (in fact, no one should, that's the optimal way of assuring that you will be true to your experience). Frankly, brutal honesty is critical if you want to get an accurate reflection of your emotional well-being. If you cheat, you're only defeating the purpose of trying to achieve positive emotional health and unleashing creative energy (so don't cheat).

The emotional inventory or diary is a tool from which you can get a clear picture of your emotional nutritional content. Your record will reflect the status of your psychological nutrition; that is, how psychologically nourished or malnourished you may be.

After you complete the 7-day snapshot, we bet you'll be surprised by what you see. You may never have realized that you felt a particular emotion as often as you did, or which people or events, or even times of the day, provoked negative or positive emotions.

Like anything else, when people are requested to offer an assessment of something, if they are not sure of the answer, they frequently respond to what they believe is "an educated guess." What does that really does mean? Well, they think they're answering the question with a guess that's based on their experience or knowledge; they also may think that their response is correct; or perhaps what they think someone wants to hear. Or, they overestimate or underestimate.

This why we are often wrong when we make an educated guess. For example, ask people how many calories they think they consume a day. They'll probably guess a number that is far from close to the actual number unless they are calorie counting. Ask people how much money they spend in a week— the same thing—they'll give you an educated guess, and may be quite surprised to find out how far off they are from the actual amount. They may have forgotten about a check they wrote or money that was automatically withdrawn from their bank account to pay bills. Most people are not obsessive in noting the frequency of their behavior and reactions.

Why is it important to understand myself like this?

Cognitive behavioral psychologists have long noted that our thinking impacts our feelings that in turn impact our behavior. Many of our thoughts are "distorted" in that we may be inclined to catastrophize, jump to conclusions, may be geared towards pessimistic interpretations; all of these reactions can cause one to feel discouraged, depressed, and depleted. A 7-day snapshot brings into focus how you have emotionally spent your week. It is a process of self-evaluation that is critical to developing the dynamic you.

Typically at this point in "self-help" books a list of instructions that is typical of psychological "interventions" may be offered to "fix" the problem. For example, if your are feeling bored with your job, learn learn a new skill or take on more responsibility to challenge yourself. Or, if you can't think of ways to change your job, then take on more demanding tasks in other areas of your life, such as: engage in behaviors during your free time that are new and exciting for you. We're not going to give you these types of suggestions. Instead, we want you to take an investigative approach: just as you look in a mirror to make an assessment of your physical self, this emotional inventory will be a process of taking mirror to you inner psychological self.

When you don't do this type of assessment, like Tina in our earlier example, you will find yourself emotionally depleted. Keep in mind this single thought: I can't flourish if I am psychologically malnourished.

A depleted state may be the psychological stated that you have been in for years. Though such a state does not feel good, you know it. Therefore, emotionally negative and de-energizing living, paradoxically, is a comfort zone that will be difficult to leave. Or, your comfort zone may not be particularly negative. It may just not be very satisfying. You have to want more than low-level satisfaction. There are psychological theories, most recently that of positive psychology, that support our contention. It is called living an "engaged life" indicating that the low-fat (positive) emotions of optimism, joy, contentment, deepen meaningful living. Staying in a comfort zone is just status-quo living; it is in many ways living the "disengaged life." Psychological nutrition, good nutrition, means that you are well satisfied; you are energized and stimulated.

Getting an accurate gauge on your emotional functioning.

As we previously stated, it is the normal tendency to overestimate, underestimate, or not even be aware of our feelings and their triggers. This is why the emotional inventory is critical. It gives you a picture of who you are emotionally and how you relate to your world. The ultimate purpose of the diary is to inform you about your emotional responsivity and whether you think you're healthy (psychologically nourished) or deficient (psychologically malnourished) in some areas. Most importantly, this assessment gives you a window into seeing how many of your moments are depleted by high-fat emotions or energized by low-fat emotions. A diary represents a means by which to assess who you are now, who you want to be, and where you want to go. After charting your emotional status, you can then see yourself. Are you satisfied with the picture? Are there aspects you'd like to change? Are there emotions you'd like to increase or decrease? Who is the person you'd like to be? For instance, do you find that you're more anxious than you'd like to be? Are you too afraid to take risks? Do you find that generally you feel bored with some of your relationships or job and want to experience more excitement or challenges? You can assess if you're satisfied with how you feel about your interactions with others as well as your reactions to the circumstances or events you encounter in your life.

Whatever your response, you'll have a better idea of you. Once again, be candid with yourself. If you ignore the data, fudge it, or not take it seriously, naturally you won't get a good picture. A moving hand taking a photograph results in a much different and less accurate image than a camera held still. We want you to take a clear picture of yourself.

Why?

Not just to feel good. That's step one.

Not just to improve your relationships. That's step two.

Not just to improve your satisfaction with your life. That's step three.

No, we want you to do this to be able to move into the spectacular: to break out of the mediocre, good-enough, same old moldy mold. We want you to prosper, to move into that flourishing, blossoming, ascendancy that will be your life. Wow. Yes, indeed.

Let's get back to the assessment of your emotional diet. To give you an idea of how this diary works, let's look at a few moments in Diane's life.

Diane is a real estate agent who works for a small company. She is 50-years-old and lives with her husband, Fred, her 14-year-old son, Jeff, and her 17-year-old daughter, Emily. Diane's widowed mother lives a few miles away, and Diane visits her every morning on her way to work.

For illustrative purposes, instead of evaluating Diane's emotional health over a 7-day period, let's just consider a very short time span.

Diane's Day

5:00 am to 9:10 am:

Diane wakes up feels tired (-)

She then drinks some coffee and feels more awake (+)

Diane goes for a run and feels energized (++).

She sees her neighbors on her way back home and has a friendly chat with them, and feels happy to hear that they are well (+)

Her husband is awake. She greets him, and feels affectionate and they kiss (++)

Before she gets dressed for work, she weighs herself and feels upset because despite watching her diet, she hasn't lost weight (−)

She vows to eat healthier, foregoes the blueberry muffin for low-fat yogurt and fruit, and feels good (+)

Her 14-year-old son comes into the kitchen before going to class, grunts a "hello" to her, grabs a granola breakfast bar, and runs out. Diane feels sad because she misses the time when he was her little boy (-).

Her 17-year old daughter, Emily, enters the kitchen. She kisses her mom hello, and looks beautiful. She's peppy and smiling. Diane feels happy and proud (++)

Emily complains about not having been allowed to buy an expensive handbag and then whines. Diane feels irritated (-).

Before going to work, Diane drives to her mother's to check in on her. Because her mother can be a complainer, Diane feels anxious during her drive there (-).

Diane also realizes that her mother is lonely and enjoys seeing her (+).

Let's add up the number of positive emotions: 7

Let's add up the number of negative emotions: 5

So by 9:10 am, Diane is at 58% to 42%, with 3 double positives (++) and one double negative (–).

Let's look at a little more of the day: At 9:10 am, Diane sees her mother who is mad that Diane won't take her to the grocery store right then, and Diane feels frustrated (-). Diane tells her that she will pick her up after work and take her shopping; when her mother says "ok," Diane feels thankful (+). Diane now gets stuck in freeway traffic, and decides to take city streets which are also jammed. This only makes her feel even more anxious (–). She wants to call her office to tell them she'll be late, but her cell phone dies and she realizes that she left the charger at home. She now feels helpless (–). She knows she will miss an important meeting with a client, and feels upset (–). She gets in to work, calls the client, and apologizes; she feels relieved (++) when he understands and they make another appointment. Diane has a lot of emails to read and feels a little overwhelmed (-), but she is able to catch up on her emails and feels calm (+).

Let's add up the number of positive emotions: 3 (38%)

Let's add up the number of negative emotions: 5 (63%)

So now by 10:45 am, Diane's at 38% positive low fat emotions to 68% negative high fat emotions, with one double positive to three double negatives.

Let's say Diane recorded the entire day. We won't go through all the details, but let's just say the work-day had more negatives than positives, (including double negatives). She has to multi-task with picking up her daughter and mother, and then taking them to events and shopping. She also has to prepare dinner and remind her children to tidy up the house because guests are coming over the next evening. Diane has a minor disagreement with her husband over financial issues, and goes to bed worrying about money and feeling exhausted.

Psychological Nutrition Assessment : Diane's Day

Time	High Fat (de-energizing)	Low Fat (energizing)
5:00 am to 9:10 am	58%	42%
9:10 am to 10:45 am	38%	63%
10:45 am to 1:30 pm	70%	30%
1:45 pm to 4:15 pm	70%	30%
4:35 pm to 8:35 pm	80%	20%
8:50 pm to 10:20 pm	71%	29%

When Diane looks at the various feelings she experienced on that day, she'll be able to see how many positive versus negative feelings she had, under what circumstances or with whom these feelings occurred, as well as the intensity of her feelings. During her waking hours, Diane had more than 50 different emotions with almost twice as many being negative than positive.

The picture of Diane's emotional state may be surprising or confirming to her. Most likely– surprising. No wonder she feels drained. We engage in a knee-jerk way in negative emotions. They become the "go-to" emotion. For Diane, this diary should be the impetus to take stock of her emotional reactivity. It will allow her to assess if she's satisfied with where she is or if she wants to make changes. A snapshot of one day from 5 am to 10:20 pm suggests that Diane was operating in the negative numbers: she is psychologically malnourished.

What circumstances or relationships she chooses to change are up to her as well as the way she decides to make these changes. The psychological nutritional label should be her key to this understanding. In examining Diane's diary, much of it falls into the realm of energy-draining emotions. The nutrient content is low.

Spoiled psychological products:

Constant worry over financial matters. Diane would benefit from reducing the intensity of her worrying about financial matters. The worry is a "junk" emotion that does not ease the financial situation. In fact, it may get in the way of coming up with a solution.

Reacting to every obstacle. We've all had startle responses: something scares us and our sympathetic nervous system goes into the alert mode with rapid heartbeat, rapid pulse, and so forth. Emotionally reacting to every irritant is like a startle response. If you startle emotionally all the time, you wear yourself out. Reacting to minor irritants of life over which Diane has little or no control, such as freeway or road traffic, is something she should toss out the window

Wanting to change others. Diane has a critical eye looking at her daughter and son. She wants to change them. But, the season of adolescence is something that her children will go through and move on; there is no need or benefit for her to become over-controlling and reactive to their moods/demands.

Getting rid of these reactions will open the way to experience more joy and self-satisfaction in her life. It can also free up time to engage and incorporate the things that make her feel happy.

Detailed Emotional EKG (for the detail oriented individual [okay, we'll say it: obsessive])

Some of us are naturally oriented towards a detailed analysis. The term "obsessive" is often used pejoratively; but, if you can't see the forest for the trees, attention to detail can improve self-understanding. If you are a data person, then you may benefit from completing an extended diary that also covers a one-week period (holidays and weekends included). However, with such a diary, you will record more details about your behaviors and emotions. The format we propose is a method that psychologists might construct if they were attempting to "quantify" emotional reactions.

Using this method, not only will you record what feelings you experienced, when they happened, what triggered them, and how you rated them, but you may also want to record how long these feelings lasted (e.g., a minute or two, an hour, and so forth). In addition, a very helpful piece of information to record would be, "what did you do in response to the way you felt—did it help, did it make things worse, did it have any effect?" Again, using this more detailed approach does require you being a bit more attuned to yourself. However, the extent of your recordings is totally up to you.

The More Detailed Approach

Time	Trigger	Emotion	Amt Time	Value	Response Emotion
8:00 am	traffic	frustrated	4 min	6	deep Breaths relaxed
8:30 am	songs on CD	energized	10 min.	2	keep Singing Happy

So, the categories used in the "Detailed Approach" are:

1.) The emotions you felt (whatever they are).
2.) What time it happened.
3.) What precipitated it (names and situations included).
4.) How long the emotion lasted.
5.) How would you rate the emotion? For example, you can use a 7-point scale, where 1 is "highly positive," 2 is "mostly positive," 3 is "somewhat positive," 4 is "neutral," 5 is "somewhat negative," 6 is "mostly negative," and 7 is "highly negative."
6.) How you responded behaviorally; and
7.) How you felt after that.

In essence, you are undergoing a "detailed emotional EKG" where you carefully monitor your emotions and reactions throughout your waking hours. If you choose to record these details, you may discover how long your emotions lasted, or that when you encountered a certain person or situation, you often acted in a particular manner. In addition, you may see a pattern in how your behavioral reactions to certain emotions tend to result in particular feelings. For example, whenever you feel frustrated about an event or a person, and respond by meditating or getting some fresh air, you feel much better.

Let's say you decide to use this detailed format. For illustration, let's look at Diane and the time period from 9:10 am to 10:45 am.

If we wanted to chart a more detailed version of this time frame for Diane, it might look like this:

Time	Trigger	Emotion	Amt Time	Value	Response Emotion
9:10 am	Mom	frustrated	2 min.	5	take her later thankful
9:15 am	traffic	anxious	20 min	6	no cell phone helpless
9:35 am	miss Appt	upset	10 min	6	calls client relieved
10:05 am	emails	upset	10 min	5	answers Mail calm

If Diane decides to complete a more detailed diary of her day, she may discover how she reacts to various situations (e.g., work, freeway traffic) as well as her interactions with particular people (e.g., family, clients). She can also see how long those reactions lasted. Finally, she can see the nature of her emotional reactions following her behavioral responses (the last column). In this illustration, she was able to turn almost all of her negative emotions into positive ones.

Diane isn't that different from other women her age. She's been busy being a good wife, mother, and daughter. She's been taking care of the house and her family while working at a job. She is concerned about her family, career, finances, and health.

The little time she spends for her physical and mental well-being is when others are occupied with their activities (e.g., sleeping) and not in need of her. She sacrifices willingly for those she cares about because it's who she is. However, as we outlined above, there are a number of expired psychological products that she is consuming. The question is, how long can she do this before their toxic effects overwhelm her?

The risk of consuming products that are spoiled is that Diane will miss out on discovering her passion and growing her creative potential. Going through each day where the negative outweighs the positive is psychological malnutrition. To be a happier and more fulfilled person, as well as more centered and capable of offering even greater support and nurturance to others, Diane needs to be living in a psychologically healthy zone, that means understanding and doing what leads to feeling fulfilled.

Grow Up rather than Down.

Recall the emotional pyramid, and the term that many mental health professionals and others use-- that of "self-actualization." The term typically signifies to realize your full potential—"to be all that you can be." Self-actualization can be accomplished by unleashing your creativity and deriving meaning in life. Recall too that we **upended** that pyramid content and put the **self-actualizing needs first**. This is something you will need to do, but something that will be a shock to your psyche. Why?

From the moment of conception, we are growing and developing; every day we move in the direction of achieving milestones. Eventually, we get to a point where we might think we have grown as much as we can and come to feel that our life or we ourselves are stagnant. We don't expect much more of ourselves, our circumstances, or our relationships—and so we just EXIST.

In fact, many middle-aged people are led to believe that whatever development we have left, may now be moving in a negative direction (e.g., losing our mental faculties, having less physical strength, becoming less resistant to infections, etc.). This type of thinking is a toxic psychological product.

We want you to reframe this: you are not losing strength, you are gaining it. Don't concentrate on the news reports that say getting older means getting weaker. Don't focus on the general sense that life and plans are for the young. Don't make negative predictions for your life, because they will come true. Make a confident prediction. Say that you are strong, healthy, vibrant, and full of excitement for what the day and the rest of your life have to offer. These statements nourish your psychological energy. You are what you perceive. This has been shown over and over in multiple studies- it even has a term, "self-fulfilling prophecy."

Yes, the body does change with age. So, some of these physical and mental conditions may be an accurate report of what happens biologically. But you are more than biology. And, it is not inevitable that emotional health will decline with aging.

In fact, it should not.

With age one acquires experience, accomplishments, and wisdom. Middle-age in our careers and personal lives signifies a very fertile phase of life where we can unleash our creative selves. By this age women have worked hard to meet life's demands (e.g., our basic survival needs for life, our financial and personal security, our family/social affiliation needs) and are now at a time and place where we can explore untapped or underemphasized creativity goals.

Fear is a high-fat emotion that will be the primary barrier to thinking in a self-efficacious way. It may be scary to think about doing something you always wanted to do, but couldn't because of a variety of obstacles.

Recognize this: the biggest obstacle is *you*. It is your interpretation of what is possible for you that limits you.

Yes, you can come up with innumerable excuses, reasons, examples, philosophies, theories for why that isn't true. But it is. You and your life are exactly what you perceive.

Many years ago a psychologist did an experiment with dogs placing them in an environment where they were shocked and had no way to escape. Then the shock was removed. Most of the dogs did not even try to escape: they knew they were defeated. But some of the dogs, a small percentage, did. See, if you define yourself as "shocked and overcome" when opportunity knocks, you won't answer the door. Why? In your shocked and defeated world, there is no door to open.

We can think of a number of examples of how fear has kept people chained to failure and mediocrity. Some women become so preoccupied with the minute details of life that they do not give their full energy and attention to the opportunity that presents itself. They prioritize picking up the laundry, getting gas for their car, grocery shopping—doing all of this instead of stopping and concentrating on the opportunity. Many times the opportunity is disguised. It may be something like a project that you are working on, and a colleague wants to discuss a new idea. You don't have the time because you need to pick up milk from the grocery store. It turns out this person then goes on to develop a great new way of doing X. It catapults that person into a whole new career. You could have been part of that. But, you put buying a gallon of milk over opportunity. See how this works?

If not now, when? Opportunities also have expiration dates. Now is all you have, so now is the time to do it.

What's keeping you from pursuing your dreams, from taking chances, from finding out all about who you are? One of us recalled reading an advice column about a middle-aged person who wrote that he wanted to be a physician but that it would take about 10 years of going to school and residency and by then he'd be too old. The columnist's answer was something like, "If you don't go back to school, in 10 years you'll still be that old and not a doctor."

Don't let age stop you; don't let circumstances prevent you, and don't let people stop you if you want to achieve your dreams.

Know this: you need a healthy emotional state to allow even the dream to take form. If you live in a poisonous, toxic environment, consuming expired products, you will have perpetual psychological indigestion. Ever try to come up with new and great ideas when all you can think of is slugging down milk of magnesia? That's how it is when you are nauseous from all the negativity. No new great idea can grow in that dead soil.

You can indeed develop ways to maintain your relationships and respect the reality of your circumstances. However, toxic relationships or placing yourself in needless negatively charged situations should be reassessed, and if necessary, ended or at least modified. You can choose to spend less time with the negative energy inducing folks; you can decide to put cotton in your ears (maybe even literally) so that their junk talk doesn't get into your psyche and poison you.

In so many ways, we are the master of our emotional state. However, we often behave like we are the slaves of fate. We abdicate that power to the high-fat emotions of fear, second-guessing, doubt.

How? Do we allow ourselves to be exploited, underappreciated, or taken for granted? Yes, frequently we do; and we would say it is done with a lack of awareness. Those are energy draining experiences that lead to the high-fat emotions of resentment, worry, anger, irritation, and dissatisfaction.

But it's time now for us to realize this and give ourselves the nurturance, love, and acceptance we've been so selflessly giving to others. Those low-fat emotions will add rather than drain you.

Really!! But it won't happen overnight. Just as a garden tended to with care slowly grows into beauty, so too will you.

Expiration dates are a part of the process.

Moving on from unsatisfying interactions, obligations, and relationships is never easy. It's hard to do because we believe at some fantastically unrealistic level that we should never press the eject button on people, especially family.

Guilt, fear, anger, and chronic conflict are among the signs of a "spoiled" emotional product. We readily consume such products in our relationships, even when they are clearly distasteful.

Ask yourself this: would you ever intentionally consume food that is spoiled or decades past its expiration date? No, of course not. Why? Because it would make you ill.

Why then do you consume expired emotional products?

Emotions such as frustration when someone you love won't engage in positive actions (e.g., perhaps they have a substance abuse problem, or spend too much money, or are just not interested in picking up around the house) is an emotion with an expiration date. After a while, frustration turns into irritation, which then turns into anger, which then ruins the relationship.

Sometimes you have to face the fact that the emotion of frustration is telling you that the "product" (that is, the relationship), is not healthy for you. It is toxic, just like eating raw chicken, it will cause poisoning. That frustration is your psychological immune system trying to fight off the poison. You might say, that's not realistic. I have to be the provider for my elderly mother; I can't just eject her because she causes me frustration. Frustration is a junk emotion (high-fat, de-energizing). You may not be able to (or want to) remove her, but you can eject the frustration. Or, keep it to a minimum.

Just like Tina can reject the Bundt cake and replace it with something healthy but still satisfying (strawberries with low-fat whip cream and sprinkled with unsweetened dark chocolate powder, perhaps?). We're not asking Tina to stop eating- just don't eat junk. It may be difficult to do so, but understand that it is important to have an awareness of when you have hit an emotional expiration date in regard to your relationships with someone.

Similarly, we're not suggesting that you should eliminate all relationships that cause friction. Sometimes you can't. But, just like you take precautions when handling toxic substances (e.g., gloves, mask), you can engage in the same process for toxic relationships products. Put your emotional gloves on, put on that psychological protective mask when a Negative Nelly that you can't avoid enters your psychological sphere.

Just like there is junk food, there are junk emotions. We're saying, Don't generate and consume junk emotions. Don't consume spoiled psychological products. Once you've completed your self-assessment, you will begin understand what emotional products in that psychological pantry need to be tossed. You should not consume expired, spoiled emotional products. They will make you sick. They have made you sick.

We will continue to explore this topic in the chapters to come.

CHAPTER 3

A Tool Doesn't get a Thank-you: Why Being Helpful Helen Drains You

Yvonne couldn't say that she was unhappy. But, she also couldn't say that she was happy. More like blah. Not that she thought much about such things–she was way too busy. Her work as a lawyer had shifted into expert identification duties requiring a lot of travel across the country. At work, she had been instrumental in forming key client relationships that brought her law firm clients who paid well. She was sharp, understood the complex scientific literature that the experts relied on but she never much flaunted this; instead, she used her knowledge to craft questions that her colleagues could use. Yvonne knew she could be highly effective conducting cross-examination in trials; however, she was relegated to attending the proceedings and never given the opportunity to be the lead attorney. One of the named partners in the firm had a habit of using her as if she were a law clerk or a very junior colleague: asking her to look up case precedents and summarize them for him, writing up his interrogatories, and so forth.

Psychological Nutrition

Everyone said Yvonne was as dependable and solid as the Rock of Gibraltar. Nonetheless, Yvonne noticed that she was not invited to meetings with the main players. She was a partner, but a junior one; others seemed to progress to better partnerships much faster than she.

Then there was her family. She was the classic "sandwiched" middle-aged female–between elderly parents and children in college. Her marriage had been on auto-pilot for years. But, whose wasn't? Because she was the oldest and lived near her parents, Yvonne spent most of her free time taking her parents to their doctors' appointments. Her parents were generally healthy, but given to complaining, and seemed to idolize her younger brother who did nothing for them. This would occasionally irk Yvonne, and once in a while she would erupt into a verbal tirade of accusations about how they clearly favored her brother over her. Afterwards, her behavior always made her feel childish, and so she would make up for it with profuse apologies and then spend more time catering to their needs.

Yvonne's two children had attended private schools; now she was paying ungodly amounts for their college tuition at expensive Ivy League institutions. She also paid their auto insurance and other bills, and when they came home on holidays and vacations, she did their laundry and made sure to have the food they liked well-stocked. These days even when they came home, she barely saw them as they were always with their friends. Her husband was an artist. Therefore, he did not contribute much in the way of income, but needed his private studio (which Yvonne paid for) to create his art and was frequently unable to help with household tasks. Yvonne envied his ability to be creative and secretly harbored a dream to be an interior designer. Her husband was seldom communicative, preoccupied as he was by the internal angst needed for his paintings. Her parents were focused on the achievements of her brother and his family. Even her children barely noticed her, other than to give her lists of things they needed. Increasingly, Yvonne felt that she was invisible to others.

Gregor Samsa, the character in Kafka's novella, *The Metamorphosis*, would have understood Yvonne's pain. Gregor supports his elderly parents and sister working himself to the bone as a traveling salesman, sacrificing his life and happiness for them. He believes that it is his duty to do so. Then one day he wakes up and finds that he has, literally, turned into a horrible giant cockroach. His family is revolted by him, and soon Gregor discovers that he was of value only for what he gave rather than who he was. Now as a giant insect he is a repulsive burden to them. It doesn't end well for poor Gregor. Why? Because a tool doesn't get a thank-you.

Many highly successful women, like Yvonne, are just like Gregor. Because they are task-oriented, disciplined, and reliable, they slowly become defined by what they do for others rather than who they are. They become tools in their family, work, and friendships. That is, they are a thing, an instrument, rather than a person.

Think of it this way: after you use a spoon do you say, "Thank-you spoon." We would doubt that many people do this. Why would you thank an object? It exists to be used for a purpose. Isn't that its function?

When you become a tool, others see you that way and react accordingly. No use complaining about them. It's not them; it is you. Helping others, being useful and competent are different than being a tool. Being a tool is also different from being an "enabler," a popular term to describe spouses/parents/siblings and their overly supportive roles in the lives of substance dependent family members. In that realm, the enabler is interfering with the development of independence and self-efficacy. A tool, like Yvonne, isn't doing that. Others merely see her as an object to be used. It's not cold-hearted; people are simply reacting to her in the way she has defined herself by her behavior.

How did this happen and why?

The "how" is easier to understand than the "why." The how is explained by habit. Habits are repetitive patterns of behavior. Some habits are good. Some are bad. Habits also become entrenched over time: meaning the more you do something in the same way over and over, the more it becomes deeply grooved and automatic as a response. The environment may reinforce other habits. Take Yvonne's helpfulness: recall that she gets praised for being so reliable. That's reinforcement for a behavior that may only encourage her to continue to behave in the same way.

But, frankly, behavioral conditioning is not what continues this pattern in Yvonne. After all, Yvonne has a mind. Here is where the "why" comes in; it is a more complex set of reactions that occur in her mind.

Yvonne has become a tool because she thinks like a tool. Her first impulses may be to find a way to be useful to someone because that is her self-definition. Recall too that after years of engaging in this tool behavior and thinking, she now feels as if she is a person who has become invisible to others. How does she feel? Blah.

She has become psychologically invisible even to herself. This would be a good example of emotional anorexia–she takes in very little emotional sustenance (recall that she is a giver). She has been psychologically malnourished now for years.

Let's look at the psychological nutritional content of a request from Yvonne's boss to draft questions for a junior (and charismatic) attorney who will be serving as the trial lawyer in an important upcoming case.

PSYCHOLOGICAL NUTRITION FACTS
EMOTIONAL CONTENT
  HIGH FAT EMOTIONS: 100%
FRUSTATION, IRRITATION, FEELING
DISRESPECTED, ANGER, DOUBT, WORRY,
ANXIETY, DEPRESSION, UPSET, FALSE
CHEERFULNESS AND AGREEABLITY.
  LOW FAT EMOTIONS: 0%

Now, if we also apply the psychological nutritional label to Yvonne's family life, her friendships, and her marriage, the ratio of high to low-fat emotions is likely going to fall in a similar range; that is, overwhelmingly in the energy draining negative emotions direction. This psychological malnutrition accumulates over time; it is like a poison slowly leeching into one's very being.

I thought being a giver was good. We believe there is a certain degree of confusion for women who are conditioned to do for others as a way of life. First, women tend, primarily, to be driven to be "other-oriented" in a helpful way. Second, it is true that the way to deeper meaning is by being other-centered. That is, a giving rather than getting philosophy which is a core commonality among the historical greats, exemplified by Mother Teresa. These individuals are regarded as self-actualized. So, isn't that Yvonne? She unselfishly supports her family, her co-workers, and her elderly parents. She puts the firm's needs above hers. She puts her parents, children, and husband first. All that is true.

We don't mean that selfishness and self-centeredness signify psychological well-being. But, being a tool can also mean that you move into the realm of psychological invisibility.

In Buddhism, there is the "eight-fold" path. It involves wisdom (the right views and intention), conduct that is ethical (what you say and do), and concentration (effort, mindfulness). Core values reflect these three elements of wisdom, ethical conduct, and mindfulness. They are ways of living and giving. Such values reflect the importance of giving, and represent a desire to help others, to be mindful of reality as it is, and to speak in a truthful and unhurtful way. Transcendent actions are those that are performed in a manner that is other-centered and not self-centered. These are essential elements of giving. They are also key to fulfillment. But you can't get fulfilled on a psychological starvation diet that erases you as a person.

How can you truly be other-centered when you are not a presence in the relationship? People can't interact with a tool, they can just use one. People can't communicate with a non-person.

The path of Unbeing. Yvonne snaps and yells at her elderly parents after listening to their endless praises of her younger brother who does nothing for them. Then she immediately and profusely apologizes and ups her tool behavior. Yvonne has in essence taken an eraser and wiped herself out. This is a difficult habit for most of us to detect and amend.

In Zen Buddhism, there is an interesting concept– that of the second perfection which involves both a core value (virtue) and an action (discipline). Discipline requires self-assessment. For the "path of seeing" or understanding one's worth, one has to have knowledge of it.

Sometimes when we are a tool we can't tell the difference between being a good and giving person, and being a "thing" to other people. When we become a tool, we abdicate self-worth. We start to walk on a "path of unseeing." Gregor Samsa did that and look where it got him.

In addition, we would say that the "path of unseeing" also means the "path of unbeing." Yvonne's marriage is empty because she's not a person to her husband anymore. How can a tool be a person? Her relationships with her children are likely equally bereft of real feeling as there are no meaningful interactions. Her co-workers and boss probably do not find her particularly interesting: do you find your Xerox machine to be a compelling conversationalist? See how this goes.

Being a tool robs you of your creative, dynamic self. It robs others of the joy of interacting with a vibrant, living individual.

You cannot blame others for not being grateful, loving, and kind to you when you have abdicated your personhood.

A tool doesn't get a thank-you because a tool has lost personhood.

CHAPTER 4

Distress Belly: Empty Emotional Calories and the Big Bulge

Recently there has been a focus on the "gut brain" (the ENS- enteric nervous system) where the gut and brain (CNS-Central Nervous System) have been found to communicate with one another. Researchers suggest that the ENS may have a critical and primary relationship to our moods and emotional functioning (there really are gut reactions). Researchers describe the ENS as a second brain consisting of more than a 100 million nerve cells spanning the entire lining of the gastrointestinal tract. It turns out that the directionality isn't one way as we thought-- anxiety to stomach upset; rather, stomach upset can cause anxiety. That is, the gut can trigger emotional reactions. Hence, there has been increased interest in the impact of food upon mood.

It works this way. Signals from the digestive system, from the microbes that reside there, through the digestion of food, move through the parts of the brain that control metabolism (through digestion). These then move through a complex circuitry of hormones and neurotransmitters to the brain that can trigger moods and emotional reactions. A new term has arisen, that of "psychobiotics" or "good gut bacteria" which influences positive mood states.

The Distress Belly – our theory- is the product of the ingestion of "bad emotions." It is an emotional gut– not in the lining of the gastrointestinal tract, but consisting of the "lining" of your psychological attitudinal state. It can manifest itself in two ways: as an emotional jelly-belly (carrying around emotional baggage that weighs you down, causes psychological flab, and keeps you from achieving your best) and as an actual physical belly. It comes about because of another kind of "bacteria"– negative emotions that de-energize you, that do not allow for the expression of creativity, joy, peace, alertness, and engagement. Negative emotions are akin to bad bacteria: they are constipating. Recall how good and bad emotions can either energize you or deplete your psychological reserves. Empty emotional calories are those high-fat emotions that lodge in your subconscious spirit and clog your emotional life. This in turn can lead to bad eating habits (like Tina) or bad moods.

WARNING: EMOTIONAL MALNOURISHMENT INDICATORS:

Stress/Anxiety	**Discouragement**
Guilt	**Depression**
Irritability	**Anger**

In addition, there is an extensive literature on the interactive effects of stress-initiated weight gain. Much of this involves the hormone, cortisol. The hypothalamic-pituitary-adrenal axis is core to metabolic regulation, with cortisol being released when the body perceives there is a threat to its integrity. Stress can generate this perceived threat. One example that this evolutionary adaptive mechanism triggers is food being converted to fat and stored, because the body thinks it needs to ward off starvation. How is distress related to this process? The body perceives psychological stress as a threat triggering the hypothalamic-pituitary-adrenal axis or HPA-axis (releasing cortisol most prominently) which then leads to fat storage as a protective mechanism. The relationship of weight gain and obesity to mood has also received considerable scientific attention. Depression, for example, has been associated with an elevation in plasma cortisol levels (the "threat" hormone that leads to fat storage) and increased fat storage around the abdomen.

Interestingly, just as malnutrition can impact brain functioning (which controls mood through the neurochemical activity and activity in deeply placed brain regions called the limbic system), psychological malnutrition (i.e., being in a state of anxiety/depression/stress) also impacts brain functioning. There is a large body of scientific literature demonstrating an association between anxiety, depression, and even post-traumatic reactions and weight gain and obesity. There may be an additional link to such emotional effects on the pathways regulating weight. Some researchers recently found that stressful life events among middle-aged and elderly individuals over a period contributed to increased weight circumference and the risk for metabolic syndromes (such as risk for diabetes, high blood pressure, abdominal weight gain). Let's look at two scenarios for the formation of the Distress Belly.

Distress Belly:

Jennifer had been divorced for 15 years. During that period, she was a multi-tasking wonder: working for an insurance company in middle-management, taking care of her twin boy (Carter) and girl (Camille); and navigating dating as a single mother. The twins were ten-years-old when she and her husband divorced. He moved across the country, married a much younger woman, and started a new family. Jennifer didn't necessarily feel rejected by her ex-husband; in fact, their marriage was a college romance that became stale almost as soon as they were married. It was the twins for whom she felt twinges of guilt: in divorcing they lost their dad. Although the twins were invited to their dad's home for the holidays, as well as spring and summer breaks, they did not feel comfortable in their father's new world. As they reached their teens, the twins rarely made visits to their dad's home. He became less and less of a figure in their lives as he grew more involved in his career and new family. Jennifer had some short-term relationships; however, the men either did not have children and felt resentful of her attention to them, or they were divorced with children and like Jennifer, did not have the time/energy/interest to devote to a new relationship.

Then Carter developed a rare condition that required numerous hospitalizations, medications that left him feeling sluggish and vulnerable to infections; this led to a complete change in their home. For the next ten years, from Carter's 13th birthday to his 23rd, Jennifer's life revolved around his medical care. She became an expert on his condition. Her ex-husband called, visited a few times, but other than that, it was Jennifer who did the heavy lifting. She had to keep a constant eye on Carter for any possible infection, and she made sure that the house was sanitized and visitors were careful with him. Her work suffered; she had a panic attack during a presentation, and for a period of time she was out on disability leave due to stress.

Camille's adolescence was turbulent. She was moody, given to shutting herself in her room, wore "Goth" clothing, and looked like a vampire. Jennifer attempted to introduce color into Camille's wardrobe and tried to arrange for mother-daughter pedicures/manicures–all of which were summarily rejected. In the 11th grade, Camille's school counselor called and said that drugs were found in her locker. Camille was suspended. Jennifer blamed herself for Camille's rebellion because she had been a smart and sweet girl before Carter's illness. Camille's counselor insinuated that it was Jennifer's fault that Camille was going in the wrong direction because all of Jennifer's attention was focused on Carter's needs as he was the sick child.

She sent Camille to live with her father. That turned out to be, predictably, a disaster. Camille and her step-mother did not get along. Camille ran away with a boy from her new school and purchased a bus ticket to New York. Luckily, they were able to find her (through access to her email), and Camille went to live with Jennifer's parents. It was not the ideal situation, but at least it gave Camille stability.

After high school graduation, Camille floundered a bit, working in fast food restaurants, dappling with junior college courses, while continuing to live with her grandparents. After a number of months, she started attending school full time and excelled; she received her A.A. degree and transferred to a prestigious private university in the East Coast for her last two years. Camille graduated with a degree in computer science and a minor in statistics. Jennifer was very happy and proud of her daughter. She made financial sacrifices for this to occur in that she sold some of her assets to cover (in part) the private university costs and helped Camille secure scholarships and loans.

Carter was slower in his academic progress given his medical issues. By now Jennifer had lost touch with most of her friends because there was no time in her busy schedule for socializing. Then when Carter turned 23, his condition was miraculously declared in complete remission. Two years after being reported in remission, Carter completed his first year of college and was moving forward. Jennifer continued to keep a close eye on what Carter ate, kept the home antiseptically clean, and made all his decisions. His treatments caused some brain damage in the realm of attention/focus problems; however, Jennifer believed he was more cognitively impaired than his physicians' assessment. Jennifer knew she was "hovering" over him; but, as Carter had come close to dying so many times, she thought it was just a natural reaction. In Jennifer's view, he may have been 25, but to her, he was much younger maturity wise.

Camille found a job back home on the West Coast near Jennifer. Because housing costs were so expensive, Camille returned, for the first time since she was 17, to live with Jennifer. Jennifer was thrilled. She thought she needed to make up for lost time with Camille and frequently asked her to go out to dinner, lunch, shopping, and the movies. Camille didn't seem to care much for these invitations, mostly declining them. She treated Jennifer like she was an aunt that you saw once in awhile and did not feel particularly close to. Annoyingly, Camille called her "Jennifer" and not "mom" no matter how many times this was corrected. Camille was making a good salary at her software engineering position; however, she did not contribute to any household expenses or even perform any household chores. Jennifer never asked, again feeling tremendous guilt for the fractured nature of Camille's adolescence, and Jennifer rationalized that Camille was paying off student loans. Still, Jennifer felt a growing resentment in how Camille treated their home. While Jennifer was neat, Camille was not. Camille did not seem to care that Carter needed a clean environment for his health. She had boyfriends stay overnight without asking Jennifer if this was okay (it was not). However, Jennifer did not make a big issue of this (she was fearful of alienating Camille). So she stifled her comments and stuffed down the irritation. At least, Jennifer thought she and Carter had a close mother-son relationship.

> **Just like high fat, high calorie foods don't nourish but add fat High cost emotions are high caloric items- empty emotions that weigh you down and deplete your psychological reserves.**

Carter then announced that he decided to transfer to a university near his father. Although it was Jennifer who had sacrificed herself for him during his illness, Carter seemed to want to be with his dad more than with her. While this was hurtful to Jennifer, she felt childish about expressing her feelings; after all, it was a good thing for Carter to bond with his father, wasn't it? Carter left and rarely called her. It was Jennifer who reached out to him. He never mentioned how much she had done for him. Instead it was always, "Dad this, dad that." She felt upset by Carter's lack of gratitude, but then she could not tell Carter this because she did not want to add stress to his life given that he had just recently overcome his long illness.

> **High cost emotions are high caloric items-empty emotions that weigh you down and deplete your psychological reserves.**

Jennifer felt increasingly alienated from her daughter. They seemed to be living parallel lives, with Camille being more like a roommate (and an unfriendly one at that) than her daughter.

Jennifer felt physically unattractive. During Carter's long illness, she stopped exercising and her weight crept up. Jennifer's work demands grew as she sought and successfully obtained promotions. That led to long hours and more weight gain.

> **Just like high fat, high calorie foods don't nourish but add fat around the belly; high cost emotions add fat around your emotional belly.**

Her friends were now mostly acquaintances as she had not kept up with them during Carter's illness. Her work associates were just that. Jennifer tried to re-enter the dating world but found that men her age seemed to be disinterested in her. She thought this was partly due to her weight and also her personality: she felt blah, and it showed.

Plus, truthfully, she had developed no interests other than work and her children. She frequently woke up tired, depressed, and frustrated. Her energy level was low. No matter what she did in terms of reducing her calories, and increasing exercise, the bulges stayed.

Jennifer finally decided to get a physical. The news: she was going through menopause and had a low thyroid level. She began to sob uncontrollably at the doctor's office. The doctor gave her medications for thyroid replacement, hormone replacement, and a referral to a psychologist.

The psychologist asked her to describe her life. The funny thing was that she had no friends, no activities other than work, and her life had become a routinized blank. The psychologist then asked her to identify stressors. It became apparent that her life had revolved around taking care of Carter to the point of hovering over him, losing her relationship with Camille, and losing a relationship with herself.

Jennifer was then asked to examine how she spent her time, and how she conducted her work and her relationships. Frankly, none of this was helpful. It just made her feel more depressed. Nothing was right. Jennifer stopped seeing the psychologist. Somehow, in wanting desperately to be healthy, to be happy, all she found was a black gloom that would descend upon her and turn to anger. She snapped at Camille one night, told her she was an ungrateful spoiled brat who was taking advantage of her. Camille moved out. When she turned to Carter, his reaction was distant and uncaring. Her parents seemed unaware of her trials and tribulations, took Camille's side, and made unflattering comparisons to the perfect life that her older brother led. No one it seemed was on Jennifer's side. Work was okay even though she had been passed over for promotions and increasingly believed that it was just a matter of time before she was replaced. Jennifer wanted to escape from her life. No one, it seemed, had appreciated all her sacrifices.

> Jennifer's emotional gut was constipated; she was holding onto all the negative emotions leaving no room for positive emotions.
> Her emotional jelly-belly was growing; her physical belly followed.

What were the emotional ingredients and their behavioral manifestations in Jennifer's life?

Jennifer had led a hyper-responsible life even though her psychological tank was running on empty.

End result: emotional constipation, poor eating and lifestyle, and weight gain. Recall that stress releases cortisol (that pesky HPA-axis at work again) and stores fat in the abdomen. As Jennifer aged that waist circumference grew. She gained both emotional and physical weight. It's not just poor food choices that were adding weight, but also resentment, anger, depression, and the "chip-on-the shoulders-superwoman syndrome" that contributed to the emotional jelly belly. Menopause only worsened what had been decades of psychological malnourishment- Jennifer had a Distress Belly.

Emotional constipation occurs when you partake in a diet of constantly "stuffing" yourself with what you believe are "obligations" to others, particularly family. As in Jennifer's case, family members may not be all that grateful for your sacrifices as they may believe that they do not benefit from them. You may have created a role for yourself by thinking you are indispensable, but actually, you have become an obstacle both to others' well-being and, more importantly, to your own. A happy and satisfied you who gives when needed, but also takes care of yourself, produces a psychologically nourished individual who will be a lot easier to live with.

Do we need to do this superwoman self-sacrifice dance? No! That's the whole point of this book. Remember: this is not just about ridding yourself of high-fat emotions and replacing them with low-fat emotions. It is directed toward a particular purpose– to release that inner creative drive in you. Yes, to realize fulfillment. To become all that you can be (no, it's not trite, don't marginalize this impulse, it is key). Remember, we upended the emotional pyramid. Self-actualization is what is supposed to drive you forward.

Reducing the Distress Belly: Actions to consider

The "emotionally constipated distress belly" lifestyle has adverse physical and psychological effects. You cannot break out your creative potential unless you are in this state.

You need to make yourself a priority. No, it's not selfish. It is self-sustaining. Without doing so, you will soon have no self.

Seek out people and activities that are energizing, and that lift you spiritually and emotionally.

Avoid the Helpful Helen and Nice Nelly traps. Recognize how and when people-pleasing becomes an obstacle to the development of an authentic self.

Eliminate the delusional (yes, it is) belief that you and only you can (fill in the blank) correctly. You may think that you are the only competent one, but you enable the lack of development in others by rescuing them.

Recognize this: your Helpful Helen ways have obstructed the growth of the very people you want to help. Think of how Jennifer's hovering hindered Carter's growth in our example.

You may need to eliminate the things that cause you psychological indigestion. This is where your emotional diary should be useful. It will provide you with a psychological map of what has not been working in your life and what you need to change. It will give you room to unleash and develop your creativity and open up your emotional channels for new ideas and associations.

Eliminate or reduce the ratio of high fat to low fat emotions.

Don't run on a psychologically empty tank. Make an inventory of the psychological nutrition of your daily life. If you have a chronic impulse to be hyper-responsible, recognize and manage this destructive psychological tendency.

What is the reason for hyper-responsibility?

Why do women do this? Is there an underlying reason for the hyper-responsible dance? Psychologists who study social influence suggest that there is a "normative" force that shapes our attitudes and behavior. That influence stems from a strong desire to conform to the positive expectations of others. Psychologists call this "social desirability." If you have a strong motivation to engage in behaviors that are pleasing to others, such behaviors may have the potential of being unhelpful, or even harmful, for you. Here are some examples. "Friends help one another" and if you do not help a friend who is in a state of constant crisis, then you are a bad friend. The normative push is to be a "good friend" regardless of how destructive it may be to one's psychological health. We are motivated to be congenial. That may be a good social lubricant (that is, you being disagreeable leads to negative consequences in work and relationships), but you should keep an eye on when congeniality moves into the maladaptive realm.

Jennifer's biggest stressors were her self-expectation that she had to remain in a parental and care-taking role for her adult children. The normative influence here is that a good mother takes care of her children by sacrificing her needs for them. The bad mother is selfish and focuses on herself. However, in Jennifer's case, she was operating in a zone that was not reality; indeed, her children were grown, college-educated, and gainfully employed. She just held onto the view that self-sacrifice made her a good mother, even though it was no longer needed.

Hyper-responsibility has a typical consequence: self-denial. This is especially so if your self-image is that of a generous person who enjoys giving to others. Self-sacrifice may exhibit itself as self-denial. For example, it may be psychologically more palatable to spend on others (your family) and deny yourself some luxuries. So, are we advocating that you forego paying bills to spend money on yourself?

No, we're not suggesting that you use the mortgage money to pay for a weekend spa retreat. (And, isn't it interesting how the objection to pampering often takes forms in such ridiculous hypotheticals)?

You would never do this. You know that.

Self-denial is a mindset formed when you are at the bottom of the priority list. Conduct this experiment: for one day put yourself at the top of the priority list. Interestingly, you will find, as we did, that once you engage in taking care of yourself you become a lot nicer person to be with. Why? Self-denial is a souring agent. And you being easier to be around is an excellent benefit to those around you, especially your family: your emotional sourness taints everyone's psyche.

A positive low-fat energizing emotion is one where you believe that you are worthy of pampering, worthy of taking care of, and worthy of indulging. Don't second guess yourself.

For many of us overachieving types, delaying gratification is the norm. Being taken care of is for others – not for me – is an idea that is hard to shake. Actually, you are not delaying gratification; what you are doing is eliminating gratification. In fact, that style can lead to pushing away help and also feeling guilty for having any times of vulnerability. The fact is, all humans need pampering.

The Dalai Lama once wrote about a "Policy of Kindness." He was describing a philosophy of treating others with kindness; yet, all too often we do not have a policy of kindness towards ourselves. In some ways, we believe we should behave according to Puritanical standards where self-deprivation is a sort of badge of honor. However, when such deprivation causes the "collateral damage" of hurting those around you as well as yourself, it is a badge of dishonor.

The Great Awakening. Jonathan Edwards, a colonial theologian in the 18th century, gave a sermon on July 8, 1741, to his Massachusetts congregation. That sermon, "Sinners in the Hands of an Angry God," became widely studied. Edwards' intent was to awaken his parishioners to the horrors of hell and what would happen if they did not rectify their sins. The sermon was said to exemplify the theology of the Great Awakening. We bring this up not for theological purposes, but as an analogy. Many of us live our lives as if we were condemned to mediocrity. Edwards awakened his parishioners by describing them as "sinners" and that they were held in angry hands.

Psychological Nutrition

Over-responsible, over-achieving women like us may unconsciously, or perhaps even consciously, hold this view: that we are sinners when we pamper ourselves, that only through self-denial and deprivation, and through care-taking of others, can we redeem ourselves from angry hands. The angry hands in this case are not those of God, but our own punitive superego. We set high standards of behavior for ourselves that negate individuality and a panoply of expression.

The "typologies below" represent insincere ways of behaving with others. Genuine niceness, kindness, and concern do not create stress, resentment, or anger.

See if you recognize yourself:

Nice Nelly: a Pollyanna smile and superficial niceness, although inside you are seething because you feel insulted or think you are getting the short-end of the stick. Nevertheless, you continue to be pleasant because being nice is what counts. You don't want anyone to call you "not nice." (this has the added benefit of everyone saying, "she's *so* sweet—" translation: she is a pushover").

Helpful Helen: Pathological helpfulness that comes at the cost of your psychological presence. You have a tendency to put others before you, but internally you feel invisible. You've put others first for so long, that you've forgotten who you are and what you want.

Simpering Sally: You often engage in phony-baloney apologies after you explode; then you go overboard in making up for this genuine expression of feeling.

Care-taking Carol: A corollary of being chronically involved in taking care of others: family, friends, co-workers. You often feel underappreciated and wonder why this is the case.

Passive Pamela: You've become invisible by your behavior of remaining in the background, not speaking up, you don't want to make waves; you just keep your head low, and agree with others on what they want to do.

Go-along-to Get-along Gail: A close friend of Passive Pamela. You make sure you avoid any conflict, give no personal opinions, keep neutral, change your tune if need be. Do whatever it takes to get along.

Busy Beverly: You immerse yourself in frenetic activity, projects and goals, and timetables and schedules that effectively eliminate all the fun from your life. This activity will allay your anxiety: if you can schedule it, you can control it. Then fast-track all your "busy beaver behavior" so that you drain every drop of romance from your life– fun from your friendships, creativity in your work, etc.

> **We need to have a vivid picture of the Hell we create for ourselves and others when we become so wound up in self-sacrifice, so much so that in reality we are not useful to anyone.**

These personalities and drives, which over-involved women have in large quantities, are maintained because we falsely believe that they represent sacrifice and are reflective of giving, generosity, being a source of calm, or a person of kindness. They are not.

In each of these cases, self-annihilation will be the end result. Eventually, you will burst, and it won't be a pretty picture (and we've seen it).

Is it any wonder that the Distress Belly occurs?

Is it any wonder that our psychological flab shows itself as a sour attitude?

Isn't it any wonder that the only true friend we really have is that Bundt cake?

> **We will see the Distress Belly melt away as we become energized so that the physical one will as well.**

We need a Great Awakening. We need to have a vivid picture of the Hell we create for ourselves and others when we become so wound up in self-sacrifice, so much so that in reality we are not useful to anyone. If we do so, then we will see the Distress Belly melt away and become energized so that the physical one will as well. What we mean is this: take care of yourself emotionally and soon you will be taking care of yourself physically too.

We've all heard this: accept yourself as you are. This is a profound truth that we need to embrace. Each of us has a physical body type as well as a psychological type (some call it temperament). Therefore, comparing and contrasting ourselves to others as to how we should be will only prolong both bellies. An oak cannot be a pine tree. A gopher cannot be a jaguar. All have their unique value. Recognize that physical change occurs. This is not a bad thing, just a new thing. Psychologically, it may mean letting go of the body type you used to have in your 20s and 30s, and embracing the body-type you have now. It may also mean letting go of the insecurities and high-fat emotions you held when you were young and immature. Perhaps it means a wake-up call to yourself; an awakening. Awaken to this noble truth: You are full of great potential. Your goal should be: Size Spectacular.

CHAPTER 5

Ejecting the Crone Myth

Several years ago a friend who was then in her forties made this observation: she was starting to feel invisible. The "pretty girl" discount that she used to get was happening, alarmingly, less frequently. She had been (and we thought still was) a very attractive woman. Her beauty had been her "calling card" that she used to ease her way into professional opportunities, as men liked to talk with her and naturally this led to valuable contacts. Various men, such as the clerk at the grocery store, the waiter, or the bartender, who would be extra attentive now barely noticed her. Then came the ultimate blow: a man of about 30, instead of flirting with her, called her the dreaded, "ma'am."

The memory of this friend's comments came up when one of us was walking down the street with a male friend and heard him refer to a young woman as a "chick," as in "that cute chick that works in HR..." The proverbial light bulb went off: that's what must have happened to our friend when the man called her ma'am: she was no longer the cute chick.

This comment led us to contemplate this vernacular:

If young women are chicks, what are older women? Hens? Hags? Crones?

Who is a chick?

When does "chickdom" end?

Does it end?

Can a 70-year-old be a chick?

Are there 20-year-olds who aren't chicks?

Are all middle-aged and older women in hagdom?

Is a young woman, no matter in what state of disarray, always a chick?

If there are chicks, aren't there non-chicks?

Does that mean that an older woman is not a chick? Is it one or the other?

The lofty posture: We don't believe that women see themselves as either hags or crones, they just may not see themselves as chicks. Often, when a man calls a woman a "chick," it typically means a young woman who dresses and acts in a certain way. Chicks are not necessarily wise, sophisticated, confident people. In fact, women who are older than 35 or so, may not want to be viewed as a "chick"– let alone called one. Women may also believe the term is disparaging. Let's look at the terms for poultry as they age: they start out as chicks, and then they become chickens, and finally are called hens (or capon). Also, by using men's definition of chicks, do middle-aged women actually choose their appearance on what they think men might like? No. Generally, their dress and appearance is to please themselves or to impress other women. Yes, they want to attract men, but their appearance is often driven by their desire to feel good about themselves. A woman wishes to look good because that contributes to her self-image and how she comes across to others. We're not "chicks"–which in actuality does have a "youth connotation," and we don't think women should aspire to be so.

The harsh realities: But there is no denying that a longing for eternal youth may be an unconscious human drive among women and men. Consider the search for the "fountain of youth," the middle age crisis (generally equated as a male "manopause" occurrence). Women, however, remain more vulnerable to the negative attributes accorded to aging; particularly, as it relates to our faces and bodies. We may not want to acknowledge that wrinkles on our face bother us, or that gravity is exerting an inexorable effect on our bodies. Moreover, if concern about our outer appearance is only within the purview of "outliers" (those self-indulgent and obsessed narcissists whose sense of self is wholly defined by the external), why then is there such a large and burgeoning skin care industry? Why are there so many different makeup products? Why is almost all of it directed toward women? Older women? If no older woman is actually concerned about having dark circles under her eyes, or having deep crow's feet around her eyes and parentheses around her lips, then how are these businesses staying afloat? They remain in the black because women buy them. Women buy them to look good and young(er). We are also influenced by an ideal of beauty that is lodged in myth more than reality; these are the archetypes.

Archetypes. Psychoanalyst Carl Jung long ago identified what he labeled to be universal images or ideas culled through the ages and stored in the human unconscious and passed down from generation to generation, which are present in the individual psyche. Some of Jung's concepts were derived from mythology and understood in the individual through that which emerged in the dream state. This review is an overly simplified rendition of Jungian thought. But, the essential element relevant to psychological nutrition is this: we can become prisoners of psychological myths. Examples of familiar archetypes are the shadow (our dark side), the shaman or spirit guide, and the anima/animus (male/female). There are also two frequent archetypal figures who occur in myths. These include the maiden (whose sexuality is generally first identified as a virgin, but in modern culture represents the sexy chick) and the wise old woman (who is either asexual or for whom sexuality is considered unseemly).

One way that archetypes have been communicated is through fairytales. Think of Sleeping Beauty: the older stepmother is depicted as vindictive and jealous of the maiden. Or, think of Hansel and Gretel: the old woman is a devouring and cruel witch. But, you say, these are stories for children. They don't influence us as adults. But they do. These stories or myths remain influential in our psyches. We tend to equate beauty with the maiden youth and relegate to the older woman the status of "crone" or old witch. This crone archetype in turn, unconsciously influences our sense of our attractiveness as we grow older. The fairytale archetypes are everywhere we look: in movies, in ads, in fashion, in music, in the arts. So, we should be aware that these powerful archetypes remain robust. They continue to suggest that a woman's usefulness, vitality, and beauty diminish as they age.

Even if the older woman is not depicted as evil, she may be marginalized (old beggar woman) or have a small and defined role (e.g., cookie baking grandmother). Older women in the mythical tales are "sidebars" not the main event. It is these two, the lithe young maiden and grizzled old woman, who we believe may form the conflicts that women face as we age.

These archetypes feed and promote the struggle to understand our beauty and sexual appeal because we are bombarded by maiden-driven images. We believe that it is this maiden archetype that may drive some women to want to look like a "chick" long past the parameters of "chickdom."

Inner beauty: is it real? But, what about inner beauty? We hear that inner and outer beauty are linked- how does this manifest itself? It is true that there is a connection between how we feel and how we look (i.e., it is how we convey who we are that influences the beholder). We've all seen an older woman whose sweetness makes her glow. Yet, it is difficult for us to believe this with any degree of confidence because we may be unconsciously (and consciously) influenced by the mythological archetypes of the beautiful young princess and the mean old witch. Many women have succumbed to these stereotypes. We do this when we feed ourselves the negative images: that as we are older, with wrinkles and the not so slender reed like a figure of the young, we are not attractive. We tell ourselves that to be attractive, we have to recapture the maiden in us: unwrinkled, svelte, and exuding a pure yet vibrant sexuality.

Other archetypes. There are other lesser known mythical images. Importantly, these are just as imprinted in the primordial psyche but not evoked as much in modern society. We need to dig these out and bring them into the open. These other archetypes for women are: the High Priestess whose wisdom illuminates the Mysteries of Life; the Mother, who is the embodiment of fertility and the life force; the Angel who is the representation of hope. These archetypes are the ones that we believe can lead the older woman to remain beautiful. Consider Mother Teresa, we would say she depicted all three of these archetypes. It was her actions that made her beautiful, the agape- or pure love for other that imbued her spirit. Take a look sometimes at pictures of Mother Teresa–lovingkindness was her makeup, it infused her with an inner glow. She was vibrant, passionate, and involved in her good works until the end. No one said Mother Teresa was a crone; that she was irrelevant. She redefined beauty in a spiritual way, but it showed physically. The feminine spiritual aspect of being is something we will focus on in the last chapter.

What about the External You? If Mother Teresa is the model, you ask, why should the external me matter? Mother Teresa provides an aspiration of spirituality in action. We are not suggesting that inner beauty does not matter. But most of us do not live the saintly life of Mother Teresa. That is not our calling. We live in the world of being a mother, a wife, a friend, an employee, an employer. In this world, how you look does indeed impact on how you feel, because others do react to your external appearance. Some of us may have the impulse to reject the external us as superficial. We use this as an excuse to let ourselves go. It is a passivity of a sort because we don't make the effort to dress up anymore. It is the world of the "schulmpy".

Caution: Don't be lulled into complacency by the narrative of the "schlumpy" that you don't have to dress well, dye your hair, or put on make-up because you have reached that wonderfully liberating age of, "What do I care?" You do care. You know this deep down. Moreover, others care. They look, and may judge you or discount you; because frankly, they see by your external "advertising" that you don't care about or value yourself. When you do not take care of your outer self, you are highly unlikely to be paying attention to your inner self.

Let's look at it this way: Do you let your home become a garbage pit? Why should you care– remember you're old? But most of us do not extend the "I am old, and I don't have to care anymore" philosophy to our homes. In fact, you don't extend this to basic hygiene either. Why bathe? You're old, remember? No one will care. They're not looking at you anyway. They're looking at the "chicks."

We would also like to emphasize this right now: stop thinking that you are old. That wise saying, "you're only as old as you feel" has a lot of truth to it. Thinking that you are "old" invites the mindset of defeat and ill-health. It says that you no longer have to engage yourself with the world. In a dreadful way, it encourages the death of the soul and spirit by allowing for sitting on the sidelines and turning living into a spectator sport.

But, let's go back to the effect of the "crone" psychology. The myth of the grizzled old woman– irrelevant, dangerous, or asexual–still has prominence in our culture. That's the crone psychology, which we want you to reject soundly and then press the eject buttom. Don't be lulled into complacency. The crone psychology is powerful, it is insidious, and can certainly influence us and our behavior and view of ourselves. It begins, as we said in the paragraphs about abdicating self-care, by a slow loosening of concern over how we look. For some women, we use the defensive posture of defeat. We embrace the crone as who we are now. The crone psychology may lead us to think that as we get older we no longer need to focus on our appearance. Such a focus is for young women, not us.

Can we realistically break and eject the crone psychology from our mindset? Yes.

But first, we have to acknowledge that the mythological archetypes of maiden and crone are enduring because they have been woven into the fabric of our lives–from the childhood fairytales to the movies and books we read. They are difficult to break out of. However, more than ever before- perhaps because so many baby-boomers are hitting what was once considered, "old age"– there is dissatisfaction with stereotypic views of women, whatever their age. In fact, we believe that there is a flux in societal concepts of what aging means. It comes from baby-boomers (and in turn influences those younger people) who are retiring and rejecting age as defining who and what they are.

This emerging redefinition of aging offers an incredible opportunity for women to re-create the vision of beauty. We believe it should be fueled by the archetypes of female wisdom and as the carrier and embodiment of hope. That older woman will embody beauty in a different way than the fairytale maiden; it will be defined from her sense of self and not from the perception of others. Recall the story of our friend: she felt she was becoming invisible as her attractiveness to younger men was waning. But that defines beauty in the context of what a younger man thinks.

We are re-defining beauty which includes re-defining the context. In other words, it's an "inside job."

You are the beholder. There may be "crone archetypes" that have settled into your unconscious. These are like weeds in your garden; they need to be dug up and thrown out as they will only strangle what you have planted. Think about these things as you look at yourself in a mirror, and get a vision of you as sophisticated, elegant, and fun. Think about how to express this newfound beauty. It is important to recognize that "beauty is in the eye of the beholder" and that there is no singular approach to achieving it. The new context is YOU! You give yourself the pretty girl discount by affirming that you are indeed now and always will be a beauty.

Yes. Beauty *can* be re-defined by you. If you feel that inner sense of calm and being, you will glow. Remember once again: we have up-ended the content of the emotional pyramid.

Self-actualization is the base of our lives. It will prompt you to consider how to best "show yourself off." It requires inner *and* outer cleansing. It means moving from the Shlumpy Susan mindset to Sophisticated Sally, Elegant Ellen, and Beautiful Barbara. It means engaging in the discovery of how to enhance yourself. It means the expression of ourselves physically and emotionally, outside of the confines of maiden-based definitions of beauty.

Remember, we've tossed out maiden and crone as the bookends of beauty and aging. Instead, we are awakening the High Priestess whose wisdom illuminates the Mysteries of Life; the Mother, who is the embodiment of fertility and the life force; the Angel who is the representation of hope. (Don't fall into cynicism here; these descriptors sound lofty, perhaps even outlandish; that is because the maiden and crone archetypes have lodged like thorns into our psyches.)

Recognize these stereotypes that rendered the older woman as irrelevant were held when the function of a woman was her childbearing fertility. We are *way* beyond that now.

Okay, you might say: all this good. But how do I get there when I see the crow's feet and the way the bulges and ripples are forming because my body is losing elasticity?

> **Beauty can be re-defined by you. We have up-ended that emotional pyramid. Self-actualization is the base of our lives. It requires inner *and* outer cleansing.**

The outer you: when blemishes and gravity hit. Sometimes we have noticeable blemishes on our face that do not bother us, nor hinder us in any meaningful way. However, for some people, these imperfections may make us feel self-conscious. Perhaps you can hide the blemish, or maybe you can't. How you react to this is the important issue.

A few years ago, Linda had surgery to remove skin cancer on the side of her face. Despite having an excellent dermatological plastic surgeon perform the procedure, she was left with somewhat noticeable red lines (her blood vessels appearing through the skin) on her face which made her feel self-conscious. A few weeks after the surgery, she attended an outdoor wedding in Florida. She wanted to look her best and tried to cover the blemish with very expensive concealer make-up designed for that very purpose. Unfortunately, it was not designed for hot, humid weather wherein the make-up ran and couldn't be re-applied. After that, she decided that having this blemish was the least of her concerns and how fortunate she was that the cancer was discovered in time. It now serves as a reminder of the need for her to take care of her health, and to accept that some flaws can't always be hidden. It's what makes us human, and what makes us thankful.

Some of us have been fortunate enough to be thin all of our lives. Until menopause hits. Then we see how metabolism slows down; how there are droops and bulges in places that were once flat. Okay. We can't deny this. Gravity exists, and as we grow older we see its effects on our body. We lose elasticity. Our jaw lines may sag. We gain weight in perimenopause and menopause. These physical changes are difficult to accept, more so for some women than others. The bulges may become disconcerting and discouraging, especially when exercise and diet do not help. For some women, this may prompt them to consider plastic surgery. For these individuals, getting rid of the skin that is sagging under their chin shaves off some years, gives them a lift emotionally.

Where does plastic surgery fit in with psychological nutrition? Didn't we say that the glow was an "inside job"? How can that possibly be part of self-actualization? Doesn't fixing what nature says is the natural progression of the body make one a superficial person?

No. It is not necessarily self-involved, narcissistic, unseemly, a money-waster, or any other negative term you can think of to engage in these "upgrades." It may have the effect of boosting your confidence.

If you've rejected the old archetypes, shouldn't you be embarrassed, be secretive, and feel like a hypocrite when using surgical means to look like a maiden?

We want you to consider this self-evident truth: it's your body.

At every juncture remember: you are a grown-up woman allowed to make decisions for yourself. Low fat emotions include self-confidence, self-assurance, and no endless second-guessing and doing what you think others will find acceptable.

BUT you must perform "due diligence." Do not plunge into these interventions. Your research may lead you to conclude that they are not necessary. If you do engage in these procedures: Do not go overboard. To be psychologically healthy and glowing, a 50-year-old woman need not look 25.

The fountain of youth can be imbibed through energized, passionate, fulfilled living; that is ultimately an internal process. Yes, the external is important (that is, you should take care of yourself physically, make the effort to dress well, care for your skin, your body), but recognize that you cannot turn back the hands of time. Nor should you want to. We have all seen people who went overboard in trying to cling to youth. It looks unnatural and unflattering to have that smooth, stretched, and non-descript face. You should take careful inventory of your psychology: are these external surgical changes really necessary for a sense of well-being?

Cognitive distortions. Here we will take a side-bar into the construct of "cognitive distortions" that psychologists often raise when considering thinking patterns that create problems. One is that of "emotional reasoning:" thinking with feeling rather than reason. We bring this up here because your face may be perfectly wonderful, yes, wrinkles and all, just as it is. Emotional reasoning may drive you to think that the face that tells the tale of your life is "old and worn" and prompts you toward excessive plastic surgery, the type that smooths away "you." This is what we want to caution against. As in all things: moderation. You cannot erase away all the years, and really, you shouldn't want to. We are suggesting that for some women, small changes may make you feel better. You don't want to become "Frozen Frances" with a flat and non-reactive face. Anything of this magnitude remains a very personal decision and one that should be undertaken with careful thought and consideration. The outer you should be glowing, but take note: it has to be in concert with upgrades to the inner you.

Hormonal changes in the realm of perimenopause and menopause can create mood changes, metabolic slowing, hot flashes –these are endocrinological facts. Still, let's not disparage our emotional fluctuations; women are often emotional beings in an emotional world and that's not a bad thing. It's a good thing. We value good hearing, eyesight, the sense of taste and smell, and proprioception; so, why not the sense of emotion? Perhaps more than these other senses, emotions have the most potential to be a "sixth sense." Perhaps when our emotions stand up on end they are telling us something we should be paying attention to. The hormones may stimulate emotional shifts- moodiness, irritability, depression that are most certainly problematic.

However, that hormonal zap may also unleash surprising creative potential. It may heighten your sensitivity to others; the dysphoria may provoke deep philosophical thought or even your own works; the hunger jags may turn you into an extraordinary cook. It may be a wake-up call that your life has been on auto-pilot and now is the time to change.

Getting older does not mean that you no longer have to focus on your appearance. The human body is beautiful in its complexity, in the delicate synchronization that has to be in effect at all moments for it to function smoothly.

> **The fountain of youth can be imbibed through energized, passionate, fulfilled living.**

This work of creation is something to be celebrated, not denigrated. Paying attention to your skin, your hair, your body and keeping it in shape is healthy narcissism. It is caring for the vessel given to you to traverse this earth by whatever way you define a universal force. It can be done without having to become a caricature of someone dressing "too young" or with multiple plastic surgeries that bleed away any of the character and depth that living life sketches on one's face.

Internally, this means recognizing those lesser known archetypes: of the High Priestess whose wisdom illuminates the Mysteries of Life; the Mother who is the embodiment of fertility and the life force; and the Angel who is the representation of hope.

Yes, that is you. It's not just poetic speech or flowery words. Keep these images in the forefront of your mind; this is a low-fat emotion that we want you to consume. Be the beholder of your beauty: look in the mirror and call yourself the embodiment of the triad of the feminine divine: wisdom, fertility, and hope.

Again, it's not silly. These archetypes are within you. Think of your life and what you have given birth to (from children to ideas). Wisdom: think of what lessons life has taught you (your inner wisdom) and what you have achieved (your fertility) and how you have passed these on to others (hope), how you are now allowing them to change and move you toward further growth. These archetypes create vibrancy in life; they are not energy drainers as archetypes of "maiden" versus "crone" can be.

Maidenhood is a season in one's life. Just like autumn is a season of beauty, winter a season of rest, spring a season of growth, and summer the season of play. Each has its purpose. So too does aging. That's the internal development of your psyche which can form and shape you in this journey of your life.

Ultimately, you will have to work at beauty from the inside out. You are not only what you think, but what you do. There is much more to come in the last two chapters about this. Remember, we have upended the pyramid to make self-actualization the base; that is the essence to psychological nourishment.

CHAPTER 6

Psychological Staleness

Staleness is easily detected in food. Think of stale bread, stale potato chips, stale cake: in every instance the food item will not be very pleasing. Staleness means a loss of the flavor or texture that gives that food its unique taste. Psychological staleness is similar in this regard: it means you have lost your flavor or your crispness. How does this happen? It happens when we stop growing psychologically. Why do we do this? Perhaps, because we have grown lazy, we've settled. Or because we fear change– because new action may mean disappointment or failure. To change may mean having to evaluate yourself and your life, and possibly, confront unpleasant findings. To change is to take risks. If you are afraid to do so, you may resort back to your life on auto-pilot.

In our book on harnessing optimism and moving toward change, *Totally American,* we wrote of an incredible young woman whom we read about in a local newspaper. She is neither mediocre nor mired in staleness. This young woman is paralyzed from the neck down. Her passion is following a professional baseball team and writing about them.

She set up her own baseball website where she provides commentary; however, the web address is not at all user friendly, and hardly anyone accesses it. The only way she can use computer is with a pen in her mouth, pecking at the keys; so, each story takes a painfully long time to write. At some point, this young woman reads an article by a major newspaper sportswriter to whom she writes telling him how his observations and analysis are all wrong. The sportswriter ignores her letters and probably chalks them up to some grandiose, curmudgeonly crank. But the young woman persists, sending the sportswriter more of her scathing remarks on his analyses. Eventually, her keen observations catch his curiosity, and he looks her up. He starts communicating with her. Then he arranges to meet her. He has no idea about her disability, as she made no mention of it in their email correspondence. The sportswriter finds her living in a remote rural area in a trailer with her family. She is locked into a wheelchair, has a pen tied around her forehead, and pecks at the computer to write her thoughts. The sports writer is stunned, awed, and captivated by this young woman's persistence. He is also touched by her circumstance and personal story. He is moved to help her create her own website for her team's fans. He writes about her in his column. Now, lots of people access her website. She's is now a bonafide professional sportswriter. Clearly, this is a woman who did not resign herself to a disability and give up her passion.

Opt for passion in your life. Don't always take the safe, easy route. Don't let a fear-driven mentality rule you.

In *Totally American,* we explored the concept of psychological stagnation. We suggested this visual: Imagine yourself at a train station. As the train approaches, you hear the conductor call out, "Next Destination: Stagnation. All Aboard." You get on the train of stagnation and follow the tracks leading to nowhere. You ride that train until the wheels fall off. You've given up control over your life and let routine be the conductor. Routine tends to produce stagnation. Getting stuck in mediocrity is living life in a "stagnant" state. It can be a zone where you are either fully entrenched or skirting the outer reaches of it. If you're trapped in that stagnant zone and live your life in a routine way, it's going to be difficult to pull yourself out of it. So, when you find yourself on the edges of "Town Stagnation," beware. That is, BE AWARE of where you are and how easily this can be a place where you go in and never come out. But there is a risk in leaving the routine life. If you venture out of this zone, you become vulnerable to disappointment or let downs. It puts you in a position of risk. Why are people afraid to venture out of this zone? Is it fear driven or is it something far deeper?

We may cling to sameness because change reminds us that all things end- including our lives. Some call this an "existential crisis." Staleness becomes the psychological comfort zone, a sort of defense against that crisis. Homeostasis is equilibrium, when the pluses and minuses cancel out one another. In homeostasis, there is no change. In flux there is. No disappointments or let downs lead one to getting stuck in mediocrity. Think of the difference in freshness between a rapid river and a still pond. To stay fresh you may have to push the envelope. Opt for passion in your life. Don't always take the safe, easy route. Don't let a fear-driven mentality rule you. Don't be afraid to try something new even if it doesn't work out. For some people, the worry is that they will come up short, and think that other people will say, "See you shouldn't have taken that risk." This is a defeatist attitude. You are letting fear get in the way of dreaming.

Another way to look at taking chances or trying new things is that there are no failures, just consecutive approximations to success. This means that you will eventually get where you want to go if you keep putting one foot in front of another. You need to challenge yourself and take chances. Transform your whole mindset, plant it in your mind that you want to do it, you can do it.

You may see others taking bold moves in their lives: leaving a staid job to venture into their passion. Sometimes when we see others do this, we may be tempted to cling even more to our safe routines. Or, we may feel twinges of envy. Do you know women like this–stuck in a routine but who are envious when others take risks and succeed? Why don't they just take the risk themselves? It may be a combination of fear and also, having tried something and failed due to a lack of persistence.

Frankly, a lot of failure boils down to not having "stick-to-itiveness" or simply the discipline to succeed. Psychologists who study how people change their behavior suggest that it takes a willingness to move out of automatic or habit-based responses into new ways of doing and being. Thereafter, in order to get where you want to go, you have to keep moving. Simple, isn't it? If you want to go shopping, first there is that desire, and then you have to make the effort to get to the mall. Thinking about the mall, dreaming about the route there and never taking one step forward, won't cut it. Same thing for your moving out of auto-pilot stale living to a vibrant life.

You have to have both: the passion or desire to be successful and a willingness to act; as well as the ability to get up and try again (maybe time and time again) when you fall down. When you are trying to achieve your goal, your passion, or desire, just know that you may hit a roadblock or two along the way; but, keep remembering that there is a pot of psychological gold at the end of the rainbow.

If you are happy with your life and who you are now as well as the course your life is taking for your future and who you will be at that time, then this information will ring hollow for you. You've already done this, you've moved out of psychological inertia into what energizes you. But, if you feel psychologically stuck, lethargic, frozen, dull, or disengaged, then how did you get there? Did you simply look at your life as a routine and give short shrift to introspection? Or, were you aware of your psychological state but afraid to step out of the routine? Both introspection and change can be scary; but, if you don't do these, you and your life will remain psychologically stale.

Ejecting fear and doubt from your diet. When you begin to move towards growing, looking for a new path, you are engaging in the antidote to staleness. It means that you will have to move off that easy, well-traveled road. To combat psychological staleness, you will have to overcome your fears, including that of failure and self-doubts about the new venture.

How?

Accept that these twinges are evolutionary throwbacks to when new things trigger a flight or fight response. Don't be a prisoner of the sympathetic nervous system that initiates these reactions. You have a highly developed cortex and regions of the brain that are geared to override primitive fear with reason.

> **When you are trying to achieve your goal, your passion or desire, just know that you may hit a roadblock or two along the way; but keep remembering that there is a pot of psychological gold at the end of the rainbow.**

Disappointments or failures are just part of the process of growth. In fact, we would say that disappointment that is more than a momentary reaction becomes a high-fat emotion. Certainly, it is natural to feel disappointed when something you planned did not work out, but that should be a small dash of emotion– like tabasco.

When something doesn't work out it is actually a learning opportunity. In fact, another way to look at "failure" is that it may provide you with what you need to move to the next step. In fact, many so-called failures are learning tools. Think of the classic example- a toddler taking her first steps. You don't expect her to immediately know how to walk, she has to fall and bump herself, but she keeps trying until one day when she stands up and walks.

Interestingly, we are actually biologically set to do this, to explore and take chances. Human beings are programmed to be inquisitive and to take risks, to look around with curiosity and interest at our world. We are programmed for adventure, not stagnation. Think of our ancestors through the course of time and how they were nomadic.

Change enlivens us. Stagnation makes us stale and BORING. Curiosity propels us forward. If we did not have that curiosity there would be no fire, no tools, no light bulb, no planes, no Internet–in short, no adventures or inventions.

Psychological staleness comes from a lack of awareness of self. Living on auto-pilot does not require discipline, it does not require self-assessment, it is the path of "unseeing." In order not to become stale, to move forward with vibrancy, one has to engage in self-analysis.

Endurance In Buddhist philosophy, the concept of endurance speaks to this aspect of the human condition: we all suffer set-backs in life. In Buddhist thought there are three levels of suffering. The first is the sensory or physical perception of pain. The second is the suffering of change. The third is a profound concept– that suffering is related to a lack of enlightenment. How does one develop endurance to suffering? You may have to develop a tolerance for set-backs, for discomfort. Tolerance means that achieving a vibrant life will not happen overnight. You may have to develop forbearance: an ability to tolerate and grow from the curveballs that life throws at you. Psychological staleness may occur because we fear the suffering that may accompany change. We duck the curveballs by staying in one place. We're not going to try to move beyond home base. This is a danger zone, inviting helplessness and negative thinking. Change is key to keeping psychologically nourished. It may be painful at first, but the key is in not allowing negative, defeatist emotions to take the upper hand.

Barbara is a woman in her mid-50s who has held the same job for 25 years, been married to her husband, Steve, for 28 years, and whose adult children are working and living on their own. For many years, Barbara and Steve spent most of their free time attending their sons' school and athletic activities. Barbara enjoyed being with her family and talking with other parents at their sons' games; but, she was always reluctant to cultivate friendships among people she knew. When her children became older and moved out of the house, Barbara's socializing diminished because there were no more of her sons' activities to attend; however, she did not feel a sense of loss about this. She and Steve adapted to their newly found free time by renovating their home and re-landscaping the yard.

A year ago, Barbara was given a generous severance package when the business where she worked was sold. She and Steve decided that they could afford for her to retire. Since then,

Barbara has stayed at home and developed new hobbies; namely, quilt making and gardening. Occasionally, she attends classes and talks related to her hobbies. Recently, she met a woman at the quilt store who spoke enthusiastically about a rare quilt exhibit in a neighboring state. While Barbara felt a twinge of excitement about this and an interest in seeing the exhibit, she eventually decided not to go because Steve couldn't take time off from work and she was afraid to travel alone. Other similar opportunities to attend garden tours were declined because Steve couldn't attend and Barbara did not want to go by herself.

As you can see, Barbara is a woman whose socializing has either been limited to family or acquaintances. Her activities tend to be with her family, at work (when she was working), and the hobbies she engaged in at home. She has gotten into a groove where she may not be as stimulated as she would like to be. Consider her interest in wanting to see and learn new things; yet, her fear of doing so alone (despite her ability to talk to others, including strangers) has stymied her.

There is nothing necessarily wrong in wanting and enjoying being a home-body, or socializing primarily with family. But Barbara is paying a price for this. Her fear of venturing out alone for longer than a shopping trip to a local establishment is stifling her curiosity and impeding her education and growth. Is she content with her life as it is or is she resigned to it? Only Barbara can answer this question. If she is content, her psychological growth may be of a kind that she accepts. But is she "submitting" to her fears at the cost of feeding her curiosity, knowledge, and esthetic needs? If so, then she is hindering herself and encouraging psychological staleness.

The amotivational state. Psychological staleness comes from an erroneous belief that staying as you are conserves psychological energy. Yet, it really is, what psychologists call, an "amotivational state." Taking risks means you might fail. Yet, no life is without failure and keeping energy moving in a positive direction can be difficult in the face of insurmountable obstacles or prior failures. Too often we allow ourselves to let others drain our energy. Staleness comes about because we buy into the stories that taking chances means risking failure. We believe the negative news stories that focus on losses, the poor economy, the impending financial crisis, and declining jobs. We let such negativity corrupt our hard drives. We do not guard our minds as we do our possessions. Think of what you do when you park your car– you lock it; when you leave your home– you lock it. But with our minds, we frequently keep it so open, that we let our positive energy leak out, or we allow it to be consumed by others, or have it become filled with the garbage of negative thinking. Soon, that "amotivational state" kicks in; you are fatigued, depleted of compassion, of drive, and of desire. All of this came from the experience of some "failure," a hope not realized, a rejection letter, a romantic loss, a promotion denied.

In the Buddhist tradition, there is something called the fourth perfection of energy: of not letting your inner strength be taken from you; not letting a momentary emotional reaction lead to a disappointment that defines you. In order to move away from energy draining negativity, that high fat emotion, you may need to become mindful of your mind. Thoughts set a positive or negative course. You need positive energy for creativity, optimism, growth, and opening doors of opportunity.

Lois was 51-years-old when her husband died. They met in law school and married when they both graduated. Ted and Lois had a wonderful marriage; he always supported her career choices and encouraged her to pursue her dreams to the extent that they moved to various cities so that Lois could accept promotions.

Lois thought of Ted not only as her beloved, but as her best friend. When Ted died suddenly from a heart attack, Lois was devastated. Although she had a small circle of close friends, she still felt alone after his death. To avoid feeling and thinking about her loneliness and loss, Lois delved more intensely into her work and spent very little time at home. After a number of months, the pain emanating from the "hole in the heart," began to wane and she returned to a less work-oriented life. She started to socialize more with her girlfriends and take trips to visit family or go on vacations with her friends.

Sometime after Ted died, Lois' friends encouraged her to start dating. She was still a young and vibrant woman who had much to offer. At first, Lois gave reasons for why she was not ready to enter the dating scene; but as her friends persisted, she eventually agreed to a blind date with a man who worked with her girlfriend. The date was OK—not thrilling, not horrendous. Lois went out with this man several more times, but stopped seeing him because there was no "spark." A few more dates with other men occurred; but, nothing materialized from them too. According to Lois, either the men were boring, they were sick and looking for a nurse, they had adult children who were very intrusive in their father's life, or they were cheap.

Lois soon became disenchanted with dating because she knew that she would never find another Ted. Despite feeling lonely and having her friends encourage her to have an open mind and not give up, Lois decided that meeting men and having to be "vetted" by them, as well as she having to engage in "discovery" regarding them, was not something she wanted to do. As time went on, Lois felt increasingly jealous of her friends and co-workers who were married, and who could dream and plan of spending their old age with their spouse.

Lois never accepted an invitation to go out with men nor did she pursue any romantic leads. While Lois bemoaned her "singleness," she was also reluctant to "put herself out there;" and so, the years went on. She remained a "widow" and the "hole in her heart," as well as the longing to be a "twosome" never really abated.

Many middle-aged women find themselves in a similar position as Lois. There is no rule than women have to have romantic partners throughout their adult life. The rule that does exist, however, is one that states, "Fear should not prevent you from seeking that which you want and are capable of having." Psychological health is not based on one's "coupledom." However, if a person does want to be in love; but, is afraid to venture out, or is feeling too tired, or is prone to offer excuses rather than take the risk of meeting new people with whom they may become romantically involved, then what other needs are they denying themselves out of fear or rejection or change? Are they also reluctant to go to new places or try new things?

> **Content and routinized are two different things. When you try to cling to routine you turn off creativity.**

Staleness and boredom. The primary ingredient in a stale psychological experience is boredom. Boredom is a high-fat emotion. Why? Because it is what psychologists call a negative emotional state since it is not pleasurable. The bored individual feels "blah" and disengaged; boredom often leads to passivity, cynicism, and can be a precursor to depression. In the workplace, it can lead to burnout. It may cause a marriage to dissolve. It may lead to a lack of friendships because being chronically bored may make you boring to others. Why is that?

Interestingly, some psychologists, such as John Eastwood and his colleagues, in attempting to define the mental processes underlying boredom, have labeled it the "unengaged mind." Boredom, as Eastwood and his colleagues suggest, is not a trivial issue, nor is it uncommon. We take their definition of boredom as reflective of an unengaged mind to also mean a state of passivity that leads to psychological staleness. The lack of attentiveness to either internal states or external occurrences happens when you are, do, and think the same way all the time. You are disengaged simply because you have come to rely on routine and auto-pilot living. This unengaged mind, we believe, forms insidiously; that is, it occurs slowly and accumulates over a lifetime into the habit of avoiding challenges. It leads to "settling" for your life as it is, unchanged for decades.

The effect of "settling for" is another way of describing psychological staleness. You are settled; you're not going anywhere—not up, not down. You have relegated yourself to a life too well-known; you are not challenging yourself to continue on a path of growth and discovery. Maintaining this lack of motivation and development may inhibit the extent of your psychological resources to be able to cope with the challenging events that occur unexpectedly during the course of one's life.

But I'm content! Content and routinized are two different things. Content and the disengaged mind do not occur together. Take inventory of the issue of psychological staleness in your life. Don't go into the defensive posture of making excuses for why you don't want to try a challenge. The clock is ticking. Yes, a biologic one: all of our days have a number. Especially in middle and later years, you understand this experientially: friends your age suddenly become ill, or die. We're not trying to scare you (okay, we are) but opting not to grow and thrive is fear-based decision making. Don't use contentment as the reason not to take a risk. Don't assume taking a risk means throwing all reason to the wind and acting impulsively. We don't mean that. Take a reasoned approach: look around, take inventory, then take action. Why? To counteract psychological staleness, you must introduce curiosity into your life. It's natural for humans to want to find out what's on the other side of the mountain. If human beings had no impulse for adventure and exploration where would we be? Remember, in a lot of ways this is evolutionarily built in: we are more creatures of curiosity than habit. So, you should take that to heart: you are built to roam and discover.

Yes, it is difficult to go into unchartered territory. We agree that the "new" may be demanding and challenging. Some of the ideas won't work. Changing your life mid-stream may mean both positive and negative consequences. It's possible that a new decision that you are making is wrong. You may have to re-track and re-set. But don't be fooled by thinking that doing the "same old same old" is safe or the best way to live your life. A comfort zone can be a psychological prison as you are lulled into complacency.

Engaged life. Martin Seligman, a psychologist who studies achieving happiness, writes about the "engaged life." This concept refers to having a life where you feel energized by your pursuits, and view them as meaningful. The fact is no matter how much you like your life on a steady course of no-change, something will happen eventually to upset the apple-cart: your boss retires, your husband decides he wants to quit his job, your children grow up, your friends move. When you try to cling to routine you turn off creativity. Think of how this is true with exercise: after awhile the same routine no longer challenges your muscles. Professional athletes change their routines so that they do not become stereotyped and ineffective. Doing the same thing (work, activities, social events) over and over will become routinized and ineffective (that is, stale and no longer satisfying you). Yes, routine may seem comfortable; but in reality it is the opposite– it is stifling. Growth means taking chances. It means moving out of staleness into unchartered territory.

Challenge yourself, push the boundaries. Status quo shouldn't be the norm. If people had succumbed to the notion of "can't do" and "fear driven analyses" of situations, no one would pursue new ventures. The irony of success is that you have to risk failure. Change may be painful. However, in the long run, psychological staleness is even more destructive as it closes the doors to self-growth, and shuts out the incredible in your life.

CHAPTER 7

Poop in the Soup:
Toxic relationships

L et's move on to another set of relationships that can cause one to become psychologically malnourished: toxic ones. Poop in the soup is a graphic way to visualize that some relationships are deadly to your emotional health. They are literally, psychological contaminants. We understand why it is important to consider your nutritional intake in relation to physical health. We have become somewhat conditioned to thinking about whether a certain food is good for us. Psychological nourishment, on the other hand, while vitally important to our well-being, is not on our radar. For example, do we assess the emotional nutrient value for people in our lives and circumstances? That is, do we really assess if associating with a particular person is worth it—not just in the moment—but how that interaction will affect us later on that day or a few days from now, or even longer? In other words, how many emotional calories are burned up daily?

Now let's not be Pollyanna-ish, let's be real. We put up with a lot because we *think* we have to, "she's my boss," "he's my husband," "that's my child." No one we know has gone through life without having negative experiences and encountering negative people. One important question is, how long do we allow ourselves to endure that negative feeling before we do something about it? How bad does it have to get before we speak up or take another form of action—like walking away (temporarily or even permanently)? The critical issue to consider is—how much do we value ourselves and our emotional health so as to take care and protect ourselves from people or events that are emotionally unhealthy for us.

Truth be told, a psychologically healthy person experiences a wide range of emotions; such as, happiness, sadness, joy, depression, boredom, excitement, anger, serenity, love, hate, frustration, contentment, fear, confidence, pride, shame, exploited, appreciated, and plenty more. We have a daily input of high and low fat emotions. We are not suggesting that this book will have you travelling in a perpetual state of happiness. However, once your diet of emotions is in the direction of low fat positive ones, this may well be the case.

The problem may develop if we experience too many negative or upsetting emotions and not enough positive or healthy ones to promote and sustain an emotional balance. Rather, we are saying that the emotional nutritional content should be in the + value and not the – value. Cumulatively, a "diet" of high-fat emotions will deplete your psychological energy. You will be burned out. Just as with food, you can indulge yourself (once in awhile) by eating emotional foods that aren't "good for you," (such as anger, irritation, sadness); but, don't make a habit of it, or you'll pay the price physically.

Likewise with people and events. Knowledge is power. This is why you should look at the "emotional nutritional value" of people and situations when you interact with certain individuals or find yourself in certain situations. How do you respond emotionally? Starting with "highly positive" and moving qualitatively toward "neutral" and continuing to the end point of "highly negative," where do you place your emotional reaction?

We developed nutritional labels in the first chapter. Here we reiterate: look at the person or event, as you would a box of cereal, and assess its nutritional value to your emotional health. This is behavior few of us perform. What was the composition of your interaction with the person or your reaction to the situation? For example, we may be aware that someone frustrates us, or that speaking in front of an audience scares us, but seldom do we fully explore the positive and negative emotions that these people and situations evoke. By looking more fully at the interaction, we may discover that we felt good about it a little later after we realized how composed we remained despite feeling frustrated. Or after the speaking engagement, we may acknowledge that while we dreaded it days before the event, and even felt like a "deer in the headlights" while we were talking, we recognize that it wasn't so bad, and we actually feel a bit more empowered.

But, just because a person or situation may be negative, that doesn't mean you have to avoid them. What you should do is evaluate what good ingredients you derived from the interaction/ event or how unhealthy the ingredients were for you. There's no way to guarantee avoiding all the negative people and situations that you may encounter. This is life. What you need to do is assess how dangerous or toxic that person or event is for you. And to modify your reactions. Recall, your feelings are the ingredients.

Joan is amazed that it is November 5 and that Thanksgiving is around the corner. She will be hosting the holidays. Joan knows that she has a lot of work to do in preparing her home, inviting her relatives and friends, and coordinating what everyone will bring for the Thanksgiving dinner.

Joan realizes that this is a lot of work for her, but she wants her loved ones to be together and to instill a sense of family tradition for her children, nieces, and nephews. As she thinks about the approaching holiday, Joan is reminded that Aunt Sally will be coming and the effect her aunt's presence will have on Joan and her guests. Aunt Sally and her recently deceased husband have been financially wealthy for years. While Aunt Sally has been generous in her gifts, she also expects much in return. Aunt Sally is a person who always sees the glass as half empty and is an outspoken critic on almost everyone and everything. Everyone seems to kowtow to her—not so much because of her gift giving, but because she can be quite caustic.

PSYCHOLOGICAL NUTRITION FACTS
SERVINGS: 1 AUNT SALLY
AMOUNT: 5 HOURS
EMOTIONAL CONTENT
   HIGH FAT EMOTIONS: 100%
AMBIVALENCE, DREAD, IRRITATION, GUILT
RESENTMENT, UPSET
   LOW FAT EMOTIONS: 0%
**WARNING: CONSUMPTION   OF   THIS
PRODUCT WILL BE DEADLY TO YOUR EMO-
TIONAL HEALTH. DO NOT CONSUME.**

If you're smart you avoid being on Aunt Sally's bad side. While her (now deceased) husband, as well as others, have pointed out her overbearing and judgmental behavior, her reply has been that she is the matriarch of the family and should always be respected.

While Joan and her relatives have long tolerated Aunt Sally, in recent years she has become more critical and demanding as well as wanting the family to see her more often. As Joan thinks about Aunt Sally coming to Thanksgiving, Joan begins to feel stressed. She's feeling torn. On one hand, she thinks it's important to show respect to her elders; she also wants to set an example to her children about the importance of family and tradition. On the other hand, she is tired of being criticized by her aunt and witnessing her insufferable behavior toward others. Joan does not print out a psychological nutritional label. But she should have.

Soon before Thanksgiving, Aunt Sally calls Joan to tell her that she is on a special diet and instructs Joan about what to buy and prepare for her. That afternoon as Joan prepares her shopping list for Thanksgiving, she starts to have a sour feeling in her stomach and begins to feel irritated. As the afternoon goes on to night, Joan is becoming increasingly upset.

When Joan talks to her cousin, Sue, the next morning and tells her about how her excitement regarding the holidays has started to wane, Sue asks her what caused this. Joan isn't sure, but she does mention the conversation she had with Aunt Sally the day before. Sue responds by saying, "That's how Aunt Sally is, she's always been that way, we just accept it and move on." Joan acknowledges that she's had the same attitude as Sue about Aunt Sally, that's why she can't understand why she's reacting differently now to Aunt Sally's behavior.

On Thanksgiving Day, Joan's home was beautifully decorated; she organized all the dishes she and her guests made, and impressed her family and friends as the epitome of a "hostess with the mostess." Everything seemed to be okay until Aunt Sally arrived late and began criticizing Joan and her husband for not arranging a special parking spot for her in front of the house. Aunt Sally continued to complain and then commented in front of everyone that the special dishes Joan prepared for her tasted terrible and that Joan must have used cut-rate and expired ingredients.

THE DARK SIDE OF NURTURING
We don't want to hurt the other person.
We don't want to be a bitch.
We don't want conflict.
We are nurturers.
We are peacemakers.
We are not warriors.
Cost: physical and emotional well-being.

It was then that Joan had her meltdown. She told Aunt Sally that she was a self-centered, manipulative, thoughtless woman who no one liked but had to tolerate. Joan also said that she hoped Aunt Sally dies a lonely woman because that's what she deserves. Aunt Sally was stunned and eventually said that she felt unwelcomed and left in a huff.

Joan couldn't believe she said what she did, even though she believed that every word was true. She also didn't feel good about herself and felt conflicted about: wanting to run after Aunt Sally to apologize and ask her to come back; or letting her go and feel as bad as she made Joan feel. The next morning Joan was still feeling ambivalent and confused about what she did because she didn't know if it was the right thing to do.

This story may resonate with some of you while others may never have had an "Aunt Sally" in their lives and can't relate. Although Joan expressed her genuine feelings, she didn't walk away with a sense that anything good came of it. She certainly didn't believe her comments would change Aunt Sally in any way, nor did she think that it helped her in any way.

Generally, interactions with people who are close or important to us are not simple. They engender a host of emotions. We often feel at odds in our emotions toward them; we may love them deeply but we may also dislike them intensely at times. We may feel taken advantage of by them, but we may also want to help them in any way we can. We can accept that they are who they are, while at the same time hoping they will change.

It is not uncommon for women to experience these conflicting emotional relationships. We tend to ignore/suppress/minimize/rationalize and engage in a whole lot of other defense mechanisms rather than acknowledge that, "It is what it is." We don't want to hurt the other person; we don't want to be a bitch; we don't want conflict; we may be afraid for our safety; and the list goes on.

Most women are programmed to be nurturers: to act cooperatively; to put others' needs ahead of ours; and to be peacemakers and not warriors. While these characteristics and traits are laudable, they may also come at a price which can have a profound effect on our physical and emotional health. Rather than express how we truly feel, we may look for reasons why we shouldn't feel that way.

Here are some examples:

Carrie's boss is very insecure. Despite feeling abused, Carrie puts up with his frequent demeaning statements because the pay is good.

Helen's "boomerang adult children" never help her around the house and expect her to do everything for them. She's not happy with this but at least she feels they need her.

Barbara's girlfriend, Lynn, calls her at all hours of the day and night to complain about her husband and ask for advice. Despite the amount of time spent on these conversations, the disruption to Barbara's life, and the fact that Lynn never takes any of Barbara's advice, Barbara thinks that she's being a good friend to Lynn.

These scenarios reflect situations where the other person's needs take precedence over yours. That may be okay if there's a fair exchange. But if you have to look for a justification for allowing your needs to be secondary (especially if it's all the time), then something is going to give. You're going to feel used and resentful. That does not make for a healthy relationship, nor does it make for a physically and emotionally healthy you.

The end result: psychological malnourishment.

We began this chapter, on purpose, with a disgusting visual: poop in the soup. Would you ever consider consuming such a product? Of course not. But emotional poop in your psychological soup, like Aunt Sally, are not only consumed, but consumed because you would feel guilty if you spit it out. Suppressing your needs to fulfill another's at the cost of resentment, anger, and feeling used, is another form of "poop in the soup."

Let's look at whether suppressing your needs so as to benefit another, while it may be unselfish and sold as exceedingly thoughtful (this is something we mental health types call rationalization), is it really a good thing to do for yourself and the other person? This reminded one of us (Linda) of the times she first began flying. Linda attended an out-of-state university and had to fly each time she went there and came home. She remembers when the stewardesses would announce the airline safety instructions. Linda was okay with the parts about the seat belt, the emergency exits, and only smoking in the designated "smoking rows" (yes, it was a long time ago). But, when the stewardess got to the part about the oxygen mask, she couldn't believe what she heard. Each time Linda boarded a plane, she heard the same thing, and sad to say, it took her awhile to appreciate the reason for it. The instructions not only included where the oxygen masks were located, how to put them on, and how to start the flow of oxygen; but, that if you were travelling with a child—put the mask on yourself FIRST, and then put the mask on your child. Wow!! Linda had a hard time understanding that instruction. Why would the airline tell their passengers to place the needs of a "helpless," "vulnerable," "dependent," person secondary to the one who is more capable? Yes, it is embarrassing to admit that it took her awhile to "get it." Clearly, if you try to save your child first, there may not be enough time left for you to save yourself. Would your child be able to assist you, know what to do for themselves and/or you, or have the physical strength to do it? If you were unconscious, would your child be able to follow all the emergency tasks that would be required of him/her to survive? An act that may appear self-centered, in reality, may be the most thoughtful and caring action one could perform for another.

So, all this goes back to—if you don't take care of yourself, how do you expect to take care of others? And, how do you expect to remain healthy? An emotionally and physically compromised person is not really helping others as well as they could if they were taking care of themselves emotionally and physically. Being nurturing and considerate does not have to come at the cost of subordinating yourself, or even worse, self-denial (unless you have a need to be a martyr).

Don't misunderstand. We're not advocating that you not care about others, or that you make sure that you are well-taken care of before you give to others. No. What we're saying is that you explore your own emotional and physical status, and evaluate if you believe you are in a healthy enough position that you can be giving, and nurturing, and supportive. If not, then what you may be giving may be analogous to "empty calories." You know how there are a lot of foods that may taste good, fill you up, or satisfy a craving; but, when we examine what is in some of those foods, we find there is very little nutritional value. It's okay to have them once in a while; but, if you consume too many of these empty calorie foods, for whatever reason, don't be surprised if you have to pay the price because your body will definitely register this. Similarly, if you keep doing for others at the expense of your needs, you will pay the price—you'll find yourself feeling burned out; you'll feel resentful; you may even jeopardize, unintentionally, other meaningful relationships. You will become a tool. Recall: being a tool means you have lost your personhood.

Poisonous People. Some fish have an interesting defense mechanism to repel predators: they mimic the look of poisonous creatures so that their predators don't eat them. Perhaps this is a method we should use to ward off predatory people: they will not want to "swallow you" if you look like you might be distasteful to them. For example, if you start standing up for yourself, like Joan finally did, you'll find that people like Aunt Sally will "leave" when not being kowtowed to (however, some might think Joan's delivery could have been a bit different).

Still sometimes you don't know how toxic a person is until you've been stung. Wouldn't it be nice if poisonous people carried a sign that was a warning? The reality is that some people are "not good for us." Some may never have been "good for us;" some may have become "not good for us." Regardless of whether they ever were or have become not good for us—today they're not good. Interestingly, these people do carry signs. Poisonous people do warn us, we just choose not to see the label. Joan knew that Aunt Sally was poisonous; she had "ingested her" on many previous holiday get-togethers.

You may be allergic to certain people. Once again, let's turn to food analogies. There are some foods that are outright unhealthy for our physical condition. Some people who experience intestinal problems after eating wheat, barley, and rye products may have celiac disease and should avoid foods with gluten, no matter how much they like a good piece of rye bread. Some foods like dairy, which were once easy to digest, may cause digestive problems as we age because of the difficulty we have in tolerating lactose. The treatment is to avoid consuming milk and dairy products. Some people and events are like these foods, once tolerable, but increasingly intolerable, causing psychological indigestion and cramping.

Psychological Nutrition

It's quite understandable when we continue to interact with people who are neutral—they may not necessarily meet our emotional needs, but they may also not upset us emotionally. It's like eating bland food that is neither too nutritious nor caloric. It may fill us up but it doesn't necessarily enhance or hinder our health. It's the food and folks who affect us negatively that we need to be concerned about.

Even if our past relationships with certain people were positive, there's no guarantee that they will remain so in time. Because people evolve, so do relationships. Many married couples who were once very compatible and happy now seek a divorce; sometimes, because one of them may believe they've changed and want something in a relationship that their spouse cannot now offer.

We all develop. Are we the same person we were when we were teenagers? Do we have the same emotional needs today as those we had 20 years ago? If we change, how can we not expect our relationships with others to change as well? Relationships are living, breathing entities. They transform over time due to a host of factors. They can grow stronger or weaker. They can be become more satisfying or more upsetting. Even if we loved someone deeply, from the very beginning of our relationship—like a mother who sees her baby girl for the first time after delivery—it's inevitable that the extent of our feelings will change. For example, the mother who loves her child without limit will most likely develop other feelings about her daughter as their relationship continues over time. As her daughter grows older, Mom may develop enormous joy and pride over her daughter's accomplishments—like taking her first step, learning how to write her name, graduating in the top of her high school class, getting married to her college sweetheart, and having her first baby. The daughter's feelings about her mother will also change over time. She may want her mother to know everything about her day and her feelings when she is a child; but, as she grows older, she may start to feel that her mother is too intrusive and she wants more privacy. When the daughter becomes married, she may want her mother to be her confidant and appreciates her words of wisdom.

Just as you change, so do your relationships. It's simply a fact that relationships have movement: it may be in a forward moving direction, or it may be regressive. How we respond to these changes is up to the parties involved. We're sure that all of us have had relationships that ended. We may have instigated the end or the other party did. There may have been an explanation for the relationship's demise (whether it was true or not, at least something was said) or it may have ended with no one offering an explanation. For whatever reasons, these relationships terminated because someone found them to be emotionally unhealthy. Even if one of the parties moves to the other side of the globe, there are still ways to continue the relationship if they so wanted; for example, e-mail, telephone calls, occasional visits. Is it a bad thing for a relationship to end? Not necessarily. In fact, some relationships won't end, even when they should. Those are often toxic relationships, ones that come at a very high cost to a person's health.

Clearly, physically abusive relationships should not be continued. Neither should emotionally abusive relationships where verbal aggression rather than physical is the form of assault and causes significant harm.

But, what about emotional disregard, a low level form of emotional abuse? How much should a person tolerate of that, after all it's kind of embarrassing to even call it abuse? Remember the old story of the frog in a pot? The fire under the pot is turned up, and slowly the water heats up. The frog feels the heat, but acclimates. The heat increases. The frog acclimates more. Before long the water has become so hot it is boiling. But the frog now can no longer jump out. The frog has been cooked. Like the frog, when we are in an emotionally abusive slow cooking pot, we tend to gradually acclimate to a climate of being put-down or perhaps, humiliated, or maybe just taken advantage of and being disregarded.

At first, it may only be an annoyance. Let's take this example. You work for a high-tech firm where you have been responsible for the development of several innovative software products. Your boss is a woman you admire for her confidence. She has told you many times how she appreciates that you are a team player and not someone who tries to grab attention for themself. Lately, she has been increasingly taking credit for your work- not fully- but she places her name first on all your projects' summaries. But, she also makes sure that you are protected from corporate politics.

One day, you become uncomfortable when your name doesn't even appear on an important and highly funded project, when they are your innovative ideas that may lead to the company earning a substantial profit. Your boss tells you this is so the work will get noticed by the higher ups at Corporate Headquarters, and she will share the credit once the project is "a go." You recognize that collaboration involves not just developing ideas but also promoting them. You have never been good at marketing, your boss is a marketing specialist, so you can see why her reasoning makes sense.

Slowly you adjust to never receiving credit for your ideas, and begin to believe that being part of a team is what matters.

Soon, raises that are your due don't come your way–your boss gets them. After all, she was the one whose name is on all the work, she is the one who has been flying around the country giving presentations to the corporate big-shots.

A promotion becomes available; your boss gives it to some-one else. She doesn't even think of you, because she has come to regard all your work as hers. She has long forgotten that it is you who does all her work. You feel miffed; but you stay silent, like a good girl, and continue to put in the hard work. Again, you rationalize that you are a team player, that you are all about group efforts, and if you are patient your rewards will come. You are long suffering and now used to being invisible. It doesn't feel good, but you have adjusted: after all when other departments are being down-sized your boss is able to keep her department safe. In fact, she tells you that your position has been targeted to be cut, but she was able to use her clout to keep you safe.

Then your boss gets a huge raise and promotion; she is now one of the larger corporate leaders for you company's entire Western Region. Now she has many people under her, including smart young graduates who are eager to do her work, eager to give her the credit, to be seen as a team player. Soon thereafter, your position is cut. You no longer have a job. Like the frog, you have been cooked.

In Linda's work of teaching forensic psychology, she frequently encourages her students to consider all the arguments to an issue before reaching a decision. You look at the problem from many points of view and then weigh each point as to how persuasive it is. (The degree of persuasiveness can be based on the likelihood that the point is realistic or true, as well as how important the point is). Once you fully consider all the points, then you can form an opinion.

Psychological Nutrition

Maybe this is an approach we should take when considering whether to enter, change, or end a relationship. What is it about this relationship that fulfills your needs (e.g., emotional, physical, financial, spiritual)? What needs of yours does this relationship fail to meet? Can you and the other party work together to achieve that which you need? Again, you have to approach this change of relationship status from YOUR point of view. You are the one whose emotional state is affected and you want to do something about it. Undoubtedly, if you have this discussion with the other party, don't be surprised to hear that they too have experienced negative emotions. And they are probably right. Remember, "it takes two to tango."

Some relationships are worth saving; some are so toxic that if you want to maintain emotional health, you can't continue with them at all or as they've been. To help decide what to do, you can analyze the pros and cons of the relationship, including the weight of their value to you. Let's look at Aunt Sally and Joan again. Aunt Sally is clearly a woman whose behavior can foster negative feelings in others. Joan could argue that her aunt is still her relative, and Joan highly values family. Another important point to consider is that this is simply how her aunt treats everyone and has not singled out Joan. On the other hand, Joan remembers how her stomach started to hurt even before Aunt Sally arrived to Thanksgiving dinner. Joan also admits that she is tired of remaining silent to her aunt's criticisms and demands; especially, because Aunt Sally doesn't seem to appreciate what others do for her. Joan is also aware that Aunt Sally has been a "negative" person for years, and has been getting worse. Yes, Joan recognizes that her aunt is now a widow and wants to be with her relatives more than ever. And Joan believes herself to be a good woman, who loves her family and wants to set an example to her children. Berating an elderly, widowed woman in front of her relatives and friends at a holiday where you are supposed to give thanks for your blessings, does not make Joan feel proud about how she displayed her long simmering frustration and irritation.

In an effort to deal with her emotional state and assess her best behavioral plan, Joan considers the following options and weighs their likely success.

1. Will Aunt Sally change after what I said at Thanksgiving if I don't do anything else?
2. Should I speak to Aunt Sally and apologize, explain why I said what I did, and hope she understands?
3. Should I just pretend that Thanksgiving never happened and continue to interact with Aunt Sally the same as before?
4. Should I either stop interacting with Aunt Sally altogether or put strict limits on our interactions?
5. Should I just accept Aunt Sally as who she is and learn how to not let her behavior negatively affect me?

Before Joan can choose one of the options, she has to evaluate the likelihood of how successful (both behaviorally and emotionally) the result would be if she selects one option over the others. If she thinks Aunt Sally will not change her behavior, either as a result of what happened at Thanksgiving, or if Joan apologizes, or even if Joan explains why she acted as she did, it may seem futile to Joan for her to have a discussion with her aunt and possibly endure more negative experiences. Now, while this may be Joan's perception that her aunt will not change, it's important to understand that we cannot make anyone change—they have to want to change (yes, it sounds trite, but it is a psychological fact). All the threats, cajoling, bribes, hints, affection, etc. won't work if the other party is not motivated to make the change for themselves. We cannot change others, we can only change ourselves. We may prompt the change, encourage it, assist it; but, in the end it is the other party who must want to do it if there's going to be a real change.

In our case, whether Joan's belief that her aunt won't change (regardless of what Joan does), is true or not, the one behavior that Joan can change is her own. Joan can take control over what she does with Aunt Sally AND hope that she reacts emotionally in a positive (or at minimum, neutral) manner with her aunt. If the interaction with Aunt Sally is so negative that no behavioral modification on Joan's part will expose her to significantly less distressing emotions, then Joan may have to make the decision to possibly end their relationship.

A highly negative relationship is toxic; how toxic—that's up to the one experiencing the distressing emotions. For example, Joan may want to think if there is any way she can make the relationship less toxic for her or is it just so bad that she has to end it. Part of her decision should include the value or importance in having or not having a relationship with Aunt Sally. What parameters can Joan set in her relationship with Aunt Sally that Joan will have to enforce? In addition, can Joan learn to modify her emotional reactions to her aunt's behavior? For example, will Joan limit her contact with her aunt to brief encounters, or only a few times a year, or only when they are at an event with others present? When Aunt Sally starts to say something critical, can Joan choose to either tune her out or listen but try to stop her reactions from becoming upsetting?

In the case of Joan and Aunt Sally, it appears to Joan that in relation to their interaction, it is Aunt Sally who is the toxic source for Joan. Aunt Sally is poop in the soup. Joan should not be "consuming" her. However, sometimes, you have to deal with "poop" and can do so without contaminating yourself. Can Joan learn some breathing exercises or remind herself that she doesn't have to let her aunt's negative comments affect her; worst case scenario, she can always walk away when she begins to feel upset. The entire burden of evaluating and changing her relationship with Aunt Sally falls to Joan, as it should, because it is she who wants to avoid, or at best reduce, her negative emotional reactivity. Remember: knowledge is power. Had Joan entered the Thanksgiving dinner with a printed psychological label, had she identified Aunt Sally as a toxic substance, it is likely that she would have stayed distant both physically and emotionally from this toxic source.

Another important issue to realize is that in many cases, we are the ones whose emotional state is making the relationship toxic.

Let's look at Natalie and Carmen. These two women met and became friends when they were in college; following graduation they drifted apart. After their college reunion a few years ago, they reunited and resumed contact on a fairly regular basis.

Natalie and her husband, Carl, both work and try to live within their means. They provide as much as they can for their three children, who range in age from 17 to 27. Their eldest child is engaged, their middle child attends a state university, and their youngest has been accepted to a private university for which Natalie and Carl have secured some loans. Natalie would like Carl to get a promotion at work so as to make more money; but, he's reluctant to do so because the business has had a few financial setbacks and he wants to spend as much time as he can with his children while they're still at home.

116

Psychological Nutrition

Carmen and her husband, William, have two sons, aged 19 and 24, who are in college and medical school, respectively. William is an Obstetrician-Gynecologist with a large practice. Carmen has not worked outside of the home since the children were born, but is actively involved in fundraising for local charities. Overall, she is content with her life, but would like to do more for people in need.

Carmen is a friendly person who likes to talk about her interests and experiences. Recently, she has been home alone more often because her husband works long hours and her children are away at school. Natalie and Carmen get together for lunch occasionally when both have time and no other obligations; they speak on the phone at least once a week. Lately, however, Carmen has been calling Natalie more often because she has started to feel lonely.

Initially, Natalie enjoyed Carmen's company and phone calls but now finds them to be upsetting. Natalie thinks that Carmen is a privileged woman whose family is independent and self-sufficient, while Natalie believes herself to be an overworked woman whose family is too dependent on her. As time goes on, Natalie finds herself resenting Carmen and becoming increasingly sarcastic with her. Natalie is not enjoying her conversations with Carmen as much as she used to and in fact, finds herself to be more upset after their phone calls than before their conversations. Natalie isn't sure why she feels this way because although Carmen is financially well-off, Natalie doesn't think Carmen lauds this over her.

Natalie also seems to resent the fact that Carmen has so much free time that she can do charity work, while Natalie has to work at a job in order for her family to have a good life. Natalie is able to recognize her feelings of jealousy and anger regarding Carmen, but believes she can't help it because she can't change her circumstances. Carmen has also picked up on Natalie's sarcasm and underlying resentment. Carmen tries not to talk about matters that could make Natalie feel jealous, but Carmen can't help being who she is and wanting to have a friend she can talk to.

As an outside observer in this relationship between Natalie and Carmen, it's hard to say who is having more difficulty and experiencing more negative emotions. The two women think about their relationship in terms of their needs and feelings. While Carmen decides that she is willing to let her interactions with Natalie become less frequent and less self-disclosing, Natalie decides that her feelings are too intense and negative for her to continue to experience. And so, Natalie breaks off their relationship.

In this scenario, we could agree that Natalie was the one whose situational circumstances and reactions to them (financial status, need to work) were accentuated by Carmen not having such experiences. Thus, as Natalie's stressors increased, her feelings of resentment and jealousy toward Carmen emerged and grew more intense. While Carmen was willing to modify the nature of their relationship by even diminishing her need for a true friend in Natalie, Natalie was not willing or able to alter her behavior or emotional reactions. This was a toxic relationship, but one of Natalie's making and one for which Natalie took ownership. She realized that in the long run it may have been better for her to end their interactions than risk further emotional harm to herself and Carmen. Natalie was feeding herself a diet of core envy, or that green-eyed monster–jealousy.

The aim in this scenario is to highlight that WE can be the source of a toxic relationship. It can be our own characteristics, needs, nature, etc., that are responsible for our negative emotional reactions. For instance, some people may allow themselves to be exploited, or they want to be needed, or they feel inadequate and not deserving of appreciation. And so, if someone takes advantage of them, or is highly dependent on them, or makes them feel less than they are, or not deserving of gratitude, why should such a person feel bad? They placed themselves in this position; in fact, they may not only have contributed to the toxicity of the relationship, but may have been the catalyst for the relationship turning out as it did.

Some people have toxic characteristics (e.g., ungrateful, exploitative, hostile) or gravitate to toxic situations (e.g., serious risk taking adventures). Consequently, these individuals may attract people or situations that draw on the individual's toxicity. For example, the exploitative person may tend to associate with naïve, passive people or the serious risk taking person may indulge in an obviously unsound economic enterprise. The source of the toxicity is the person and not the other individual or situation. If the toxicity of the relationship or situation originates with us, then realizing and accepting this is the first step on the road to emotional health. If we can't work on ourselves and treat that which is unhealthy, how can we blame others for our feelings?

The critical issue in achieving emotional nourishment is looking at yourself honestly, knowing who you are, and what about you contributes to situations and relationships with others that result in negative emotions.

Regardless of whether the other person or situation stimulates a negative reaction in you or whether you have toxic

characteristics that influence you to engage in unhealthy re-
lations or activities, it is you who must make the decision to
change.

Only you can work on modifying your needs and reactions
to being psychologically nourished as opposed to chronically
malnourished.

CHAPTER 8

Constipated Success: Hoarding

E ileen has spent the last 30 years in a corporate world where the glass ceiling is the rule rather than the exception. But she has prided herself on being the exception. Eileen was highly intelligent, socially astute, and knew what side of the bread was buttered. She was never a great beauty, but she dressed in a way that conveyed authority. She never succumbed to female stereotypes of cooperation; competition was what made for winning and she was going to be a winner. This sometimes meant that she befriended her junior colleagues and then tossed them out when she had no more need for them. She made sure that all ideas had her stamp of ownership. As a result, she became the CEO of a large manufacturing firm and later branched off to build her own empire. Her personal life had the veneer of success: a husband who moved in the same glittering circles, but who she saw rarely due to their busy professional lives. Although she superficially acknowledged others, as was socially appropriate to do when given awards or at corporate meetings- in truth, she clenched every one of her ideas with a tight and closed fist. Eileen was a hoarder.

A hoarder? How? This woman is sleek and successful: isn't she the picture of emotional health? Isn't she realizing her inner creative drive? We've all seen the television depictions of hoarders: homes stuffed with bags and boxes. But isn't that what the Eileen is doing? She is weighted down by her hoarded success. Her bags and boxes clutter her psychological sphere; they take the form of selfishness, of me-first, and, "If I have to step or stomp over you I will." They form meanness around her, a halo of arrogance. She is off-putting in relationships; she is charming at corporate dinners, when she can look and act as if she cares (which she does, for herself), so as to move up the ladder of success.

Hoarding success recalls a Biblical proverb: it is easier for a camel to go through the eye of a needle than a rich man to enter the gates of Heaven. Why? It can be said that the rich man who hoards gold has not opened up a resource more precious than gold: that of opening up another human being's potential and dreams. That of helping someone fulfill their destiny. It is an I-centered emotional mindset that in the end stifles the growth of the spirit. We may be able to see this more clearly in a wealthy and influential individual. For example, such a person uses a position of power to add to their already enormous wealth, or to gain sexual favors from people, instead of using their position to change the world.

The Russian writer, Leo Tolstoy, wrote short tales on morality that were generally intended to be instructive to children. However, Tolstoy's tales hold profound meaning for adults as well. In one story, entitled, "How Much Land Does a Man Need?" the protagonist, Pahom, begins with a small homestead but is driven to be better and richer than his neighbors. He is able to accrue more and more land, and engages in disputes with those around him for trespassing on what is his. Despite being rich, he wants more. Then Pahom learns from a tradesman that there is a tribe living by a river who owns more acres than the eye can behold. These people are said to be "simple as sheep" and would sell their land for almost nothing.

Pahom travels the great distance to seek these tribesmen, and finds them. He gives them gifts for which they ask him what they can do in return. Pahom responds that he would like to buy their land. He is told the price is one thousand rubles a day. Pahom is surprised by this, and learns that this means he can have as much land as he can encircle by foot in one day– from sunrise to sunset. He must start and end at the same spot by sunset, or he forfeits his thousand rubles and receives no land. Pahom agrees and is dazzled by how much good and fertile land there is.

At sunrise Pahom marks the beginning spot, digs a hole, and places a marker. All the tribesman are present and cheer Pahom on. He starts to walk off and when he looks back, he sees the tribesman gathered at the bottom of the hill. Pahom could easily loop back and make a circle of a nice portion of land. However, greed takes the better of Pahom, and he makes the circle ever larger and larger, despite his bleeding feet and almost broken stamina. As the sun begins to set, Pahom sees the hill that marked the beginning spot, and with his last breath, he runs up the hill and then falls to the ground dead. How much land does a man need? Six feet from the head to the heels to lie in.

Pahom was a hoarder.

For most of us, we may not even be aware that we have become success hoarders. We want to challenge you to open up your hoarded success bags. What can you do to release some-one's potential? Share an idea? Share your work wisdom? We may not be conscious of our hoarding. Perhaps we make our way to the top of the ladder at work, and then get so busy attending meetings and ensuring our own standing, that we fail to make changes that could have a major impact to others in our organizations. We fail to become the voice of kindness, of change, of seeing how others can also succeed.

You may say that, "I'm not Eileen; I don't have that type of power or money." Kindness to others isn't linked to being a saint all the time; it isn't linked to your bank account; it isn't linked to having special abilities or powers. All you have to do is "do it." Small acts accumulate to life changing events.

> **We may not even be aware that we have become success hoarders.**

Or maybe you do have a position like Eileen or money and you say, "I give to a lot of charities." Life offers you daily opportunities to be kind to others in ways that are personal. You may have someone in your company "low on the food chain" whose potential you can unleash. Eileen likely had innumerable opportunities to do so. Imagine the type of company she might have had if she were a giver rather than a hoarder?

Hoarding success means that new ideas may never come to fruition. It also means that by your words and deeds, you crush the creative spirit of another person. Look around. You have knowledge and skills; you can open doors for others. That's being a success sharer. Remember, being psychologically nourished means feeding yourself the food of self-actualization. That food doesn't come in packages made for one.

We've seen this in academic spheres as well; go to any large academic conference and you will see the worship of the "maven." Too often this person will be one who is puffed up with importance and will not have the time to engage in conversations with the "little people;" e.g., a graduate student. There are numerous instances where the influential person will use a student or underling to do the "grunt work" and then take credit. After all, it may be rationalized, without their significant name attached to the project it would never have received the prominence that it now has. That is another example of constipated success.

Giving is core to the first Buddhist perfection and a part of the eight-fold path. This philosophical view gives us a glimpse into why an I-centered hoarder of success loses what is the most rewarding aspect of life: our ability to give. Giving is the opposite of hoarding. Giving leads to sustained and deep meaning. Only through giving can one achieve one's higher purpose. Hoarding means that eventually, all your accrued success will lose their luster. You may gain the promotion to a position that pays well but offers you no sense of satisfaction. You may be in a relationship that is stuck in stagnation because both parties have nothing to give to one another. Your life is so routinized by selfish needs that boredom is all you feel anymore.

> **We want to challenge you to open up your hoarded success bags.**

We've written previously that finding the "big" meaning in one's life begins in the context of core values and being a part of something bigger than your own life. Hoarding is not such a core value. We've discussed the psychological concept of "self-actualization" which promotes the drive to finding an other-centered higher purpose. There are other psychological concepts which underscore this view.

Will-to-Meaning. In transpersonal psychology this has been described by Viktor Frankl as a "will-to-meaning." Viktor Frankl, psychiatrist and developer of Logotherapy, articulated the life and death nature of what he called, "the will to meaning." Frankl was born in Vienna in 1905. He grew up in the epicenter of the birth of psychoanalysis, the home of Sigmund Freud. Frankl earned a medical degree from the University of Vienna in 1930. Eight years later, Austria was under the control of the Nazis. And Frankl was a Jew. Frankl's life went from a shining career as a psychoanalyst to a concentration camp prisoner. In his book, *Man's Search for Meaning*, Frankl described how he struggled with what to do at the precipice of the Nazi's control of Vienna. He had an offer to go to the United States, but it meant leaving behind his elderly parents. One day he came home and saw his father holding a fragment of stone in his hand. He asked what it was. His elderly father replied that a Jewish temple had been blown up, and this was the remnant from a tablet of the Ten Commandments that his father happened to find. Frankl asked which Commandment; his father replied, "Honor thy father and mother." This sealed it for Frankl, he knew he must stay. And he did, only to be taken, along with his wife and parents, by the Nazis and sent to concentration camps. He never saw any of them again.

Frankl spent the next few years, from 1942 to 1945, in four Nazi camps. In witnessing the horrors, and in experiencing them himself, he came to refine a psychological theory and therapy: Logotherapy. Logos is the Greek word for meaning. Frankl observed that when his fellow prisoners lost hope, when they lost purpose and meaning to their life and their circumstances, they perished. He found that meaning was critical to sustaining life. Meaning could be derived from suffering. Even under the most adverse circumstances, life had meaning, and human beings always have the choice to find it.

What can you do to release someone's potential? Share an idea? Share your work wisdom?

Here's another example of a successful person who could have supported the creativity of another, but did not.

Eve loved her family. She had two daughters and a wonderful husband. While she always wanted to be a journalist, her circumstances were such that she accepted her role as a housewife, and decided that she'd be an excellent homemaker. She loved to cook and bake, and was always experimenting. She had a knack for putting unusual ingredients together and creating marvelous dishes and baked goods, without ever using a cookbook. One of her prized creations was a pastry that had a crisp, flaky crust, and a chocolate and nut filling surrounded by a homemade jam composed of fruits from her backyard. Not only did her family enjoy the pastry, but it was always a hit whenever she gave it to relatives and friends.

Helen and Michael were good friends of Eve and her husband, and they owned a small shoe repair business in a fashionable area of town. One day, while they were eating lunch, a woman walked into their shop and asked if they could repair the broken heel of her shoe. Helen recognized this woman immediately because she was a famous cookbook writer who frequently appeared on television. Michael said the repair would not take long, and Helen offered her a piece of Eve's pastry while she waited. Helen told the writer about her friend and how gifted she was in cooking and baking. The author ate the pastry and couldn't believe how good it was. She said that she had tasted all types of pastries during her long career and never had anything so unusual and delicious. She told Helen that she wanted to contact Eve to get the recipe so that she could include it in her next book. Helen said that she thought Eve would be delighted to share it because being associated with a famous baker would be thrilling for Eve. The woman corrected Helen and said that she wanted the recipe, but that Eve's name would not be mentioned because she'd tweak the recipe to make it her own. Yes, this woman was successful…in hoarding success.

Ego-addiction. Hoarding prevents seeking that meaning. Selfishness feels good in the moment, but in the long-run, it is an empty and lonely life. Such a person has done little to help others and has no deep connections to anyone.

The Dalai Lama describes this as "ego addiction"– a process where the self is inflated, causes suffering, is overwhelmed with emotions, and cannot find peace. When speaking of wisdom, the Dalai Lama links it to removing ego-addiction. Growth occurs in an other-centered way of living. The Dalai Lama describes the interdependence each of us has on one another's well-being. When you are a success hoarder you have effectively disconnected yourself from others. Whether this derives from a spiritual, philosophical, or psychological perspective, it is clear that meaningful goals are ones that occur in the context of a higher purpose. Fulfillment cannot be experienced in a lasting manner unless it rings the chords of deep meaning. It is more than momentary joy or exhilaration at a job well done (although you need that as well); it is by nature "other-centered" rather than "self-centered."

You may think, "I'm not the Dalai Lama or Mother Teresa. I can't do this." Here you would be wrong. Look around. There are many examples of ordinary people engaged in extraordinary acts of other-centered giving.

Recently, we read the following story: Nine women ranging in age from 54 to 72, and living in West Tennessee, literally began baking happiness by selling special pound cakes and using the proceeds to help others in need. They call themselves the "Nine Nanas." They started small, inspired by their own grandparents who always helped others in need. Their philanthropy was prompted by this question: If they had a million dollars what would they do? All of them had a desire to help others less fortunate than they. But they didn't have a million dollars. However, they did have the money to spend on sending shirts to the laundry. They decided to do the laundering themselves and keep the money. When they heard about someone needing help, like a single mom who couldn't pay her utility bill, they stepped in anonymously and paid it. They became "drive-by do-gooders:" literally driving through low-income neighborhoods to see who was in need of a good deed. They dropped off care packages, bought clothes, picked up groceries– anything that was needed. They baked special pound cakes from their grandmother's recipe and sold these to augment their funds. Until recently their good deeds remained "undercover," even from their husbands. Now their whole families are involved. Why?

The families also wanted to "give back" and "to make sure happiness happens." The Nine Nanas are examples of kindness, but also smartness. They used their talents to help others and themselves. It felt good to give. Why? Altruism it turns out sets off the neural pleasure pathway- so you do indeed feel good when you do good.

There are innumerable stories out there like this: of everyday people who step up to the plate and make the life of someone around them better. Psychological nourishment, the stuff that best feeds the soul, comes from the impulse to make a life better. That requires adding these behaviors and impulses to your psychological daily intake. Success hoarded is not success at all. It is just selfishness. It is emotional constipation. It is small dreaming. It is bottom dwelling living. Big dreaming, what we want to release in the world, requires a commitment to considering how you can sow and harvest seeds of success in others.

Years ago we read about a remarkable woman. She was living a meager life working at a low paying job that barely covered her expenses. Yet, she was deeply committed and engaged in service to her fellow man– something that stemmed from her Christian faith. Her way was to feed the homeless who congregated at a local park. She managed this by scraping together whatever money she had and soliciting left-overs from local restaurants and grocery stores to cook plates of food. Then she would leave the food outside the tents and sleeping bags of the homeless. It was a dangerous feat because that park had a number of drug dealers, and violence was the norm. Yet, this lady was never harmed. She never said a word to anyone; she just put out her food packages every day. She was clearly the polar opposite of our hoarding Eileen.

Hoarding promotes cynicism and suspicion, because one is always fearful of others taking from them.

Cynicism is easy. It does not require you to do anything.

Cynicism keeps doors of opportunities closed.

Cynicism is an impurity, something you need to wash out.

Sometimes in order to purify your behavior, you have to suppress your selfish impulse inclinations.

Ironically, by doing so you will achieve more.

You will dream bigger.

You will feed your soul.

> **Success hoarded is not success at all. It is just selfishness.**
> **It is emotional constipation.**
> **It is small dreaming. It is bottom dwelling living.**
> **Big dreaming is what we want to release in the world.**
> **Sow and help another harvest the seeds of their destiny.**

CHAPTER 9

Big Dreaming: Feeding your Soul

Big Dreams are something that remain elusive to quanti-fication because they are made of the fabric of gut in-stincts, deep desires, and stretching beyond the obvious. They have long led to human beings gazing at the stars in the night sky to consider the unfathomable, such as the size of the ob-servable universe. Is it finite? Infinite? Bounded? Unbounded? Is it spherical? Or, because, as it is ever moving, the shape of it cannot really be defined. Perhaps it is spiritual in shape and therefore not measureable by the human eye or our instruments.

Does it matter what the shape of the universe is? Why do this?

We do it because creative impulses run strong in humankind. How strong?

Albert Einstein's famous equation, $e=mc^2$ (that the amount of energy in a mass is that mass multiplied by the speed of light squared and the speed of light is a fantastically large number1:

186,000 miles/second) indicated that the amount of potential energy in a mass was enormous. This equation was later used by physicists and chemists to spilt atoms.

Similarly, creative energy is exponentially huge, waiting to be "spilt" within each of us. The creative potential that we all have is what moves us into the realm of self-actualization. It answers to many names; such as, "one's destiny," "unrelenting desire," "a strong passion," or simply, achieving your full potential.

Releasing such energy comes from Big Dreaming, being an "atom" splitter of creativity.

Atom Splitter

Bessie was born in 1892, the tenth child of African-American share-croppers in Texas. That meager beginning, or perhaps because of it, planted the seed of a big dream: she wanted to "amount to something." That dream to move from obscurity, from the ordinary to the extraordinary, was a long standing spark within her. What we would now call Bessie's "demographics" of race, gender, and poverty would suggest that her dream to rise above her impoverished circumstances (never mind "being something") was unrealistic. Her education began in a one-room school house with frequent interruptions due to the demands of cotton harvesting and other responsibilities. Nonetheless, Bessie was diligent and driven to learn, and so she became an outstanding student. She saved enough money that when she was 18, she was able to enroll in the Oklahoma Colored and Agricultural Normal University. Unfortunately, it was only for one term because her funds ran out.

She moved to Chicago. In 1916, while working as a manicurist in a barber shop her dream began to take form: she wanted to be a pilot. Her passions were ignited by the stories she heard from pilots returning home from World War I. But, the reference frame was this: no American flight school would accept her because she was 1.) A woman; and 2.) African-American.

Bessie persisted, focusing on France to attend aviation school, taking French lessons, and then finding the funds to move to Paris. In 1920, she started aviation school and a year later she earned her pilot's license. In doing so, Bessie Coleman became the first female African-American pilot as well as the first African-American to hold an international pilot's license.

Still, upon return to the United States, despite the fanfare, she realized that to make money as an aviator she had to become a "stunt flier." Then she hit another barrier: no one in America was willing to teach her to do so. Once again, she returned to Europe and learned to become an exhibition flier. She went back to the United States and performed stunts to cheering crowds. She harbored another dream: establishing her own flight school. Unfortunately, Bessie Coleman died in a plane accident at the young age of 34, never establishing her flight school; but, she demonstrated something more enduring– an example of living to realize her destiny. Bessie Coleman lived life in the "big dreaming" mode.

Big Dreaming is what we should all be doing. Big Dreaming is the best psychological food you can feed yourself. It may mean that you will have to move out of the norm. Big Dreaming to feed your soul may mean being an oddball, an outlier, but its reward is great.

Reference Frame

In physics, there is an interesting concept (for us non-physicists) to consider in the context of Big Dreams. It is that of *relativity of simultaneity*, meaning that two distinct events separated by space cannot be said to occur at the same time. For example, when observing two events (A and B) at two different geographic locations, it will sometimes appear that A came first and at other times that B did, depending upon the observer's reference frame.

From a psychological viewpoint, we think that the observer's reference frame is a concept worth borrowing (and bending) from physics and using for our own ends.

Lucy was the seventh of ten children born in New York in 1833. Lucy had a big dream: she wanted to be a doctor. But, women were not doctors at that time. So she took a route available to her and became a teacher. Lucy taught school in Michigan for 10 years. She lived the "realistic" dream of a profession open to women by becoming a teacher. Although, being a teacher is most certainly noble, and while it may be someone else's big dream, it wasn't Lucy's.

Lucy applied to Eclectic Medical College, the only school at that time that accepted women. She soon discovered that the school changed their policy and no longer allowed women. Lucy was told to try dentistry instead as it was "less stressful." Lucy apprenticed with a dentist who taught her how to pull teeth and make dentures. Despite this training, Lucy's application to the dental school was rejected. Why? Because she was a woman. Again, she was hitting the wall of how others define us and how we should live. "Dream a small dream, Lucy," they were saying, and "forget all this silliness."

Warning: big dreaming means that others may ridicule you.

Lucy did what many people never do; she picked up that big dream, tucked it under her arm, and held it firm, even after a decade of being "realistic." Others likely ridiculed Lucy's dream: she was dreaming an unrealistic dream. However, she was undaunted and persevered. She apprenticed with other dentists and received private tutoring from a professor of Dentistry. She started her own dental practice in 1861. She moved to Iowa and after three years was allowed to join the Iowa Dental Society. Finally, after gaining this professional recognition, in 1866, she was permitted to enter the Ohio College of Dental Surgery and earned her degree. Then her big dream made history: Lucy Hobbs Taylor became the first woman in the United States to earn a doctorate in dentistry. By 1900, almost 1,000 women were able to tread the path forged by Dr. Taylor to become dentists.

Big Dreaming is not only good for you; it is good for others as it has a ripple effect. Notice how in just a little over three decades after Dr. Taylor received her dental degree, other women were able to follow in her footsteps.

Today, the Lucy Hobbs Taylor Award is the most prestigious honor that the American Association of Women Dentists bestows upon outstanding women dentists. But in her time, she was clearly an outlier. Lucy Hobbs Taylor did not marry until she was 33 when she married a man whom *she* taught to become a dentist. No doubt, those who rejected Dr. Taylor's application to dental school wanted her to remain within the parameters of "what everyone else is doing." But to do so means that you have to acquiesce and allow external limits on what you can be.

From the reference frame of the male professors at the school of dentistry, Lucy Hobbs Taylor was likely an eccentric female butting her nose into areas that were unseemly for a woman, and probably unqualified to perform.

Lucy Hobbs Taylor from the reference frame of today is a heroine- a woman charting uncharted territory. Dr. Taylor chose her inner drive, her big dreaming, to be her reference frame and forged ahead.

You may think, "That's great. But I'm not like those two women. I don't have a big dream. That sounds grandiose."

Is Big Dreaming grandiose thinking?

First, let's think through why we get snared in the small dream trap. Few people dream big, or even if they do, they do so in secret and then stifle the impulse. Women are great "dream impulse stiflers." But, you might say, "This is the 21ˢᵗ century, filled with women in power, breaking that glass ceiling, conquering Wall Street, being movers and shakers." Do we still need to be encouraging a break out of the mold philosophy for women now? That's so 1970s "hear me roar stuff." Seriously, aren't we all there already? It may or may not be society or cultural values that form the glass ceiling. That debate we will leave to the social psychologists. What we know is this: It's not a matter of what century you are in. It's a matter of where mindset lives. If you believe that you are not capable of breaking that glass ceiling: you won't. Yes, you've heard this before. But, this is such a self-evident truth: why are people, and women in particular, reluctant to give voice to their big dreams?

Why? Small dreams are the norm because most of us are afraid to be viewed as silly. Women, in particular, seem to be fearful of being labeled negatively. Small dreams are called "realistic" and "rational;" in contrast, big dreams have these labels "unrealistic," "far-fetched," and perhaps even "grandiose" or "delusional." Women like to fit in, to be right there running with the herd, among the pack of the "normal." Notice the first four letters, NORMal. Fitting in with the norm is what being normal means.

Many of us may harbor this stereotype that entrepreneurship is the business of the young. We say: break out of the norm, that's the psychological glass ceiling you set up for yourself. You might say I understand. I wish I had thought of that way when I was young; or, I did develop new ideas, not its time to put myself to the pasture, let the young ones have their chance. Big dreaming is for the young. The Yupik people of Alaska had a tradition of passing down wise words from the elderly to the young. One piece of compelling wisdom was this: that those who ignored the wise words risked peril. Why would we do so? Sometimes, we are given wise words in forms that we ignore due to our prejudices. They don't seem wise because they contradict our routinized, "stay with the norm philosophy." They don't seem wise because we don't truly believe big ideas and innovations can come from those in mid-age or beyond. We say, come on, can you really break out with new ideas at 50? At 60?

Consider this. Recently, a business journal highlighted "eight at eighty," representing a group of entrepreneurs who were *starting* innovative new businesses at age 80-years-old or older. Was this a story about geriatric delusions? No. It was a story about staying in the game and not letting age define you. Their stories of new ventures with 10-year business plans may have been viewed by some as delusional.

Consider Klaus Obermeyer: that he was remaining in the business trenches even at age 94. Rather than be relegated to irrelevance, the business philosophy that sustained his company's longevity is what is a much sought after model. Obermeyer's ski-wear company was founded in 1947, and he is credited with creating the down parka by cutting a comforter and making it into a jacket. This is one among a myriad of now familiar ski accoutrements (e.g., mirrored sunglasses, high altitude sunglasses) he developed.

"Eight at eighty" were individuals who were not interested in running with the pack.

Staying with the pack and tunnel vision thinking. But, remember our fatal flaw: women like to fit in, to be right there, running with all the rest of the "normals." It is worth emphasizing again: the first four letters, NORMal. Fitting in with the norm is what being normal means. Consequently, we shut out the means to understand ourselves and one another in the process. We dismiss a path or a method because of a knee-jerk rejection: it's too idealistic, delusional, grandiose, and unrealistic; or risky. Who wants to break the mold at age 45? 50? 60? 65?

Nonetheless, you may argue that for men and women, there is going to be ageism (think of the Silicon Valley, the land of software millionaires all before the ripe old age of 30). There may be an expectation that innovative thinking is the purview of the young.

This type of attitude reflects tunnel vision thinking. Not only can it stymie growth, but it is also the artery clogging high-fat emotional diet that is toxic to big dreaming. We are so poisoned by this form of thinking that we shut the door to incredible opportunities.

Bessie Coleman and Lucy Hobbs Taylor were oddballs. They were out-of-the-norm females who broke the mold; they split the creative atom and lived life from the reference frame they defined. Breaking out of the mold is what we are encouraging. As a young person, it may be difficult to do; but, in middle-age and older, especially for women, it may seem an impossible task.

Why? Because the big dreams are buried under social appropriateness. That desire to be normal becomes a cloak that covers up your inner "unrealistic dreaming." It seeps into your bloodstream with each decade so much so that it is like a second skin. How can you even contemplate change if your work and life have been buried under the avalanche of the handmaiden psyche, infected by the mediocrity virus, or sustained by the fear-driven fungus? That's what psychological malnourishment does: it leeches you of the ability to be fully alive and creative because you are in a perpetual state of emotional starvation. No big dream will come back to you in this state, let alone, be pursued. Can you even remember what the big dream was?

Still, isn't it also true that with age comes wisdom and the ability to see more than just that which is before your eyes, both in business and in life? Those who remain fixed and rigid in holding old ideas become obsolete; those who are flexible and open to new ideas stay in the game (like the "eight at eighty").

> That desire to be normal becomes a cloak that covers up your inner "unrealistic dreaming." It seeps into our bloodstream with each decade so much so that it is like a second skin.

So, after having written all of this about splitting your creative atom to dream big, don't be shackled by your chronological age; this is not where we are stopping.

No, we have a different agenda beyond igniting you to dream big.

So, what is our point?

Entrepreneurial philanthropy

We're talking REVOLUTION. No more "testosterone-driven" female CEOs. No more cutthroat politics. No more aversive female bosses who create strife and competition. We want a feminine revolution of atom splitters of creativity. Success breeding success. Looking for new ways to help others release their potential while also releasing your own.

This fits in with the feminine nurturing spirit, the drive to be cooperative, and to respect the wise words of those older than us. We are not going to marginalize older women because this is not a "male game." We are dealing with wisdom and not virility.

We are advocating entrepreneurial philanthropy–true, those two words intuitively just don't seem to go together. Entrepreneurs are aggressive, competitive, and driven towards their profit margin. Philanthropy signifies just the opposite: cooperation, doing for others before self, generosity, and giving. Why are we linking together these two concepts in the realm of releasing creative power? Because we want to release the power of the "giving" female entrepreneur in an explosive, new way. Not just in the realm of donations for humanitarian non-profits, or toward funding academic departments or institutions. No. We are talking about the successful woman giving something she has the ability to do–open doors of opportunity for others. Not just mentoring, but doing.

We want you to be bodhisattvas of bringing the inner destinies, the dreams of others to fruition.

An interesting concept in Buddhism is that human beings can be released from suffering and find *nirvana* on this earth. Nirvana means inner peace. Imagine the ability to do so– to find peace and happiness right here in the midst of the ever present noise of a competitive, aggressive, dog-eat-dog world. But how? In Mahayana Buddhism, those who excel in the Zen practice are called the bodhisattva, or enlightened individual. Bodhisattvas have mastered six perfections (in Sanskrit called *pāramitā*): the perfection of giving, of behavior and discipline, of forbearance, of vigor and diligence, of meditation, and of transcendent wisdom. They don't stay in their insular enlightened world but *seek* to instruct others in achieving personal freedom. They're not meditating on a mountain, but sharing their wisdom.

Net-doing, not networking. We want you to share your success and knowledge. We don't want networking; we want net-*doing*. We want you to be bodhisattvas in bringing the inner destinies, the dreams of others to fruition.

Remember how we stated earlier that giving is core to the first perfection? Being in the moment and giving, to make altruism a priority is not the sole proprietorship of Zen Buddhism. Certainly it is evident in so many religions and philosophies, and in the myths of old, and in the wisdoms of the indigenous peoples, to cite just a few. We know this truth well: a higher purpose toward helping others results in sustained and profound meaning.

Entrepreneurial philanthropy is a way of giving that trumps all other types of philanthropy because you are involved in helping another person realize their inner destiny. This concept is described in psychology as "self-actualization" or in transpersonal psychology as "will-to-meaning." Whether from a spiritual, philosophical, or psychological perspective, what is clear is that meaningful goals are ones that occur in the context of a higher purpose. Meaningful goals lead to fulfillment that is experienced in a profound and sustainable way, not momentary joy or exhilaration, but an "other-centered" rather than "self-centered" will to success.

Recall, that Zen Buddhism and the "eight-fold" path involves wisdom (the right views and intention), conduct that is ethical (what you say and do), and concentration (effort, mindfulness). Wisdom, ethical conduct, and mindfulness are ways of transcendent living and giving. Entrepreneurial philanthropy is a form of transcendent living through actions; i.e., work performed in a manner that focuses on others and not on ourselves.

Isn't this unrealistic? If human minds can actually develop and comprehend an abstract concept such as the shape of the universe being described by cosmologists as 93 billion light years from any one point, aren't humans then capable of developing almost infinite imaginative possibilities? Isn't there room in that universe for a philosophy and practice of entrepreneurship based on lifting others to reach their potential? Why is that unrealistic?

How would this look? It would be a landscape of encouragement and doing: encouraging big dreaming in others and lending a helping hand to make those dreams come true. Philosophically, we want to place a value on the giving entrepreneur. Spiritually, we want to release the power of the feminine divine. Grandiose? Let's just see.

Entrepreneurial philanthropy is a way of giving that trumps all other types of philanthropy because you are involved directly in helping another person realize their inner destiny.

CHAPTER 10

The Feminine Divine: Starting a Dream-maker Revolution

All revolutions have a philosophical basis. It may not be readily apparent, but if you dig down it will emerge. Entrepreneurial philanthropy is a revolution drawn from entrepreneurial altruism. It is based on a philosophy of the feminine divine. By that, we mean the feminine divine spirit. We believe this spirit has been lost- or if it is there, it holds a second tier status in standard spiritual and religious practice. Feminine Divinity is peaceful, cooperative, nurturing, and driven toward giving birth and maintaining life rather than grounded in defeating others and destroying life.

Most revolutions have been driven by a masculine ethic, and largely the purview of men. Thus, when you think "revolution," the idea evokes images of warriors and great battles over important issues. We acknowledge that there are numerous examples of women who were integral to these causes and exhibited bravery in such engagements: female soldiers in the American Revolutionary War (e.g., the oft-cited Deborah

Samson, a female revolutionary soldier who disguised herself as a male) and during the Civil War (e.g., Harriet Tubman who actually led a military expedition to liberate slaves in South Carolina). In addition, in the 20th century, there were: Petra Herrera and the *soladeras,* female combatants in critical 1914 Mexican Revolution battles; Lakshmi Sahgal, who was an officer in the 1940s Indian National Movement, and commanded an all-female regiment to overthrow the British Raj; Golda Meir, as a revolutionary Zionist, and many, many more.

What we mean by the feminine divine, however, is not reflected in the above examples. In the realm of fighting for political freedom and human rights, Nobel Peace Laureate Aung San Suu Kyi, from Burma, called "the Lady," reflects the feminine divine. Although she was imprisoned by the junta and under house arrest for 15 years, after her release she still wanted to negotiate with her oppressors. Her proposed method was to have a friendly tea with them!

It is that cooperative impulse that we call the feminine divine. A cooperative impulse coupled with the desire to give birth and to nurture the creative potential in others

Feminine Divinity as Dream-Releasers: We're not talking political movements. We mean a movement toward releasing the destiny in others. Feminine divinity means becoming the atom-splitter by unleashing the enormous energy of another's potential. Doing so begins the dream-maker revolution. We see the feminine divine as deriving strength from this nurturing cooperation and endeavor.

It is NOT a "male-bashing" philosophy. We like men. But we are not men. We don't want to be men.

Be cautioned, however, this is not merely getting in touch with "your inner goddess." Remember, this is net-doing, not net-working. It is womentoring, meaning not just mentoring, but also doing for that person (for example, opening doors, giving them jobs, finding resources, making introductions and engaging in finding a way that others can benefit from your treasures of wisdom and influence).

Here are some core points:

We want a feminine-centric (versus male-centric) business and success model that taps into our natural desire to nurture growth.

We are programmed to be creators, not destroyers. Recurring aspects or themes of feminine divinity are Mother, and fertility–these are evident across cultures and time.

It is also **NOT** a "male-bashing" philosophy. We like men. But we are not men. We don't want to be men.

Competition is one way to succeed. We think cooperation is another means to success; the better path.

> Feminine divinity means unleashing the enormous energy of another's potential: that is what begins the dream-maker revolution.

We are going to highlight two "syndromes" that have to be eliminated from one's psyche in order to let the feminine divine flourish: the important person and Machiavellian Mary. There are others, but these two are so common and destructive to the seeds of creativity (in you and others) that they are worth highlighting.

The Important Person Syndrome. Many times we become thick-skinned to others' requests once we gain a bit of prominence. We rate people in terms of their "importance" and give time to those who can do something for us, or who are as "important" as we are. In Hinduism, there is this theme: a small child, a beggar, or a mentally impaired individual asks something of an important person, perhaps something to eat. The important person cannot be bothered by someone who is so beneath them. Then it is revealed that the unimportant person (in Hindu tales) was Krishna, the God in disguise, and the important person realizes the error of their arrogance.

This theme is surely familiar in many traditions and religions. Haven't all of us been tested in this way?

One of us remembers an event that happened to a student when he went to a conference and was looking forward to seeing one of his heroes, an accomplished mental health clinician who employed a therapy that promoted warmth and genuineness. After the clinician completed his speech, the student approached this individual and waited patiently until those before him finished their conversations with the clinician. Eventually, the clinician turned to the student and said, "Yes." The student told the clinician how happy he was to meet this individual and how much the student wanted to learn about this treatment method. The student only spoke for a minute or two (and not in too gushy terms), when the individual said, "Cut the crap, what do you want?" You can imagine how devastated the student was when he returned from the convention. His hero may have been a therapist, but this person didn't seem to follow their own practice of being warm to the student; however, maybe, the clinician was being "genuine" by showing their "true self."

Dismissiveness, rudeness, rushing someone off the phone, brushing them off, not returning a call or email are facets of the important person syndrome. They are poison to the feminine divine. Do the opposite. If you are in a position of power or influence use it that to uplift someone.

One may ask, why should we give our influence away to strangers? After all, we fought hard and worked to get it.

We lose sight that all of our inner creativity is given to us by the Divine; that our creative gifts are indeed "gifts" that should be shared.

Don't misunderstand. We are not saying that you should give away all your possessions and money, and take up residence in a cave on a remote mountain. No. Quite the opposite. We are saying if you can, make it happen for others by unleashing their potential. Help them so they too can enjoy life, can have that car, that house, and take that dream vacation.

Many years ago one of us had an interaction with a very successful author. That writer was fearful of others wanting to have access to their publicist and encroach on the author's genre. Interestingly, the writer relied heavily upon others for their time and expertise so as to give the author's work realism. It was a "give me" mindset rather than a giving one. We wonder how many opportunities to release that inner spark of creativity this individual could have ignited, but never did. How many times have we done this ourselves; hoard our success because we believe that if we release our knowledge, somehow we will lose what we have gained? Give and you grow your heart. Give and your soul too will grow.

Let's take a look at the second syndrome, insidious and devastating to entrepreneurial altruism. It is that of Machiavellian Mary.

Machiavellian Mary. Though women are inclined towards cooperation, ironically, however, once in positions of power, one may look to competition models to guide us. We think that to move up "the ladder," it requires one to be ruthless; or since that is not palatable, we soften the adjective to "realistic" or "politically aware." In fact, all the nice adjectives are just candy coating on the true nature of this syndrome. The Machiavellian Mary mentality has an identifiable pattern: a process of scheming, conniving and ingratiating to those you are important to one's gains and stepping on those who are not. Once up the ladder: the goal is to rid yourself of all your enemies.

We've been the consumers of this style ourselves, as underlings to bad female bosses. We've been the consumers of this as citizens when our female politicians adopt this type of politicking.

Machiavellian Marys can be found in positions of power across all fields. They succeed because women think that such characteristics are admirable: they are playing well in a male game. No soft and fluffy nurturing cooperation, but a hard as steel, step on and over you, approach to succeed. Such a woman knows and understands a man's world and plays the game skillfully.

But, this admiration is ill-spent and actually toxic to us all. These women are toxic substances; in fact, you could say that they are evil.

That's a strong word. But look at what Machiavellian Mary does. She destroys the creative spirit of those around her; she moves up by stepping on the necks of others; she uses strife and dissension to get ahead; she promotes an environment of distrust, suspicion, and of having to watch-one's back. She is a predator and her prey are those who represent obstacles to her success. She is ever aware of her surroundings and looks for the opportunity to strike and destroy. She creates an atmosphere that is toxic to creativity.

A Machiavellian Mary is a "backstabber" and we would say, even worse, a "soul stabber." She divides and conquers. Those who can "get along" with her delude themselves by thinking that somehow others do not understand her— but they do. Those women who serve as handmaidens to Machiavellian Mary believe that they know the "real world" of success that the things Machiavellian Mary does are necessary to succeed. Those who fall by the wayside are in this Machiavellian world, recalling the original social Darwinian term, not the fittest.

But these Machiavellian Marys and handmaidens are not familiar with reciprocal altruism. This theory of evolutionary biology (developed and generally attributed to evolutionary sociobiologist Robert Trivers) suggests that cooperation (or helping others) may have an evolutionary beneficial basis, i.e., I help you now, and later when I need it you help me.) This is alternate version of the standard competition model as related to survival of the species, or the "eat or be eaten" drives. We borrow (and bend) this term here to forward our view of "entrepreneurial altruism" as having a functional benefit not for economic "survival" but for the larger benefit of enhancing meaningful living.

So, couldn't an "adapted evolutionary theory" of cooperation also be applied to business? To academia? To any creative endeavor?

Yes. It can.

We believe that "cooperation" instead of the traditional "competition," will result in an exponential explosion of inventions, original works, scientific contributions, and successful businesses. The key will be the seed of entrepreneurial altruism. To underscore, our conceptualization of entrepreneurial altruism is not driven by the potential for reciprocity but driven by pure reward of helping or uplifting others. We believe that the *cooperative* spirit of success is the feminine divine force that can stimulate and nurtures the potential of others.

You may wonder if the cooperative spirit is so inherently rewarding, why isn't it the norm? Why is it that human nature seems to slide toward the seflish? Evolutionary biology approaches cooperative and competitive altruism in terms of what is observable: how in groups of mammals those who cooperative fare; or examining symbiotic type relationships that remain even when the usefulness of the relationships is over. None of this really helps explain- we don't believe anyway, why people stray away from the unselfish toward selfishness.

As clinical psychologists, we would say our experience has borne this obvious conclusion: human motivation is complex. Many times people knowingly engage in behaviors that they know is self-destructive. Other times, people engage in acts of stunning bravery to save strangers that they know risks their own survival. Still, there are other instances where people turn deliberately away from acts of evil as they do not want to get involved, or believe that others will help so there is no need for to concern themselves with the event.

Therefore, we may need to look at the "why of Machiavellianism" from an entirely different viewpoint than biology.

C.S. Lewis, generally known as the writer of the Narnia tales, wrote a very interesting and short novel, *The Screwtape Letters*. This novel is written as a series of letters. They are mentoring missives about how to corrupt a mortal away from good and relinquish his soul. The mentor is a senior executive, Demon (Screwtape), and the mentee, a junior demon (and his nephew), Wormwood. This work may be illustrative of why Machiavellian Mary strikes our psyches so effectively. Screwtape tells Wormwood that the path to hell is not a plunge off a cliff; but, in fact, a gradual gently sloped journey. It is full of small compromises that you sow in the mortal's mind: small seeds grow doubts with an attitude of cynicism. You slowly lead the mortal to believe that greed and self-centeredness, unbelief in a faith that can't be seen (such as religion or spiritual views), and belief in "what can be seen" (such as observable proof) are sophisticated ideas. You need to understand that the world is "dog-eat-dog" because that is man's nature. In contrast, the fool wears naïve, rose-colored glasses in viewing the world, and accepts the pabulum of religious thinking to keep themselves deluded. Fear, dissension, doubt, doing what is best for oneself right now, even if it hurts another, all promote sin, which is how Screwtape advises Wormwood to work the mortal toward giving up his soul to the Devil.

Cynicism is the weapon of the Screwtapes and Wormwoods of this world. It is a powerful force that allows the Machiavellian Marys of this world to remain robust. Cynicism tell us that entrepreneurial altruism is unsophisticated, childish, utopian thinking that only invites becoming prey in a predatory world.

See how this works? Screwtape and Wormwoods really don't have to do much to create this poisonous mindset. In order for the seeds of entrepreneurial altruism to take hold we have to deliberately dig out the toxins of doubts, cynicism, fear from our psyche. Then we can proceed to live in a world that uplifts others; one where our goal is to unleash their creative capacity.

Machiavellian Marys are anti-nurturers, they kill the feminine divine. In fact, they are the anti-feminine divine.

Reject Machiavellian Mary. Look around the Machiavellian Marys that you know or have known. When you are on Mary's good side, when she "confides" in you about the failures of other employees who are "incompetent" because they are "unrealistic" and "weak-minded," how do you feel? Special?

Beware. She is Wormwood using you; she is planting the seeds that because she confides in you, somehow you are "superior," "better" than all the others around you who have gone by the wayside. When Machiavellian Mary is at her best, you will feel isolated from others, see them as less-than, as incapable fools, while only you and Mary are the brilliant ones trying to do the right thing. Yes, she may be authoritarian, but that's not dictatorial. Sometimes you need a firm hand to guide an errant department. You slowly become her henchwoman. Others in the department are wary of you: they know any criticism of Machiavellian Mary that you hear will get back to her through you. They are afraid of you. Then, it will all change. In an instant. Just as in Lewis' tale, when the soul is turned, there is no more need to pamper it with soft words to push the mortal in the direction you want. Now that you have the soul, you can throw it on the pile and move on. This is what happens to all prey of Machiavellian Mary. We told you: she is a predator, a destroyer of the inner creative spirit. She is the anti-feminine divine. Don't become her. If you are her, throw off that cloak of suppression of others. Apologize to those you have hurt. Change your ways. If you work with Machiavellian Mary and have been schmoozing up to her: stop it! She will destroy you!

Women must reject Machiavellian Mary as a role model for leadership. In fact, we should not tolerate such Marys in our lives. We should "out her" and say, "no more." These women are anti-nurturers, they kill the feminine divine. In fact, they are the anti-feminine divine.

Releasing the feminine divine means doing the opposite of Machiavellian Mary. It means spreading your influence that others may grow. Thornton Wilder, the playwright who wrote, *The Matchmaker*, had his character, Horace Vandergelder, a wealthy merchant, remark that money was like manure, it needed to be spread around. We think that's the case for success as well. Like manure, you should spread it. Look around for how to do it. The inner female essence is giving. Release that.

If you are the female CEO of a company, what are you doing to open up the inner destinies of others? Who is out there, who has an idea or a dream that you can actually make happen? How wonderful would that be? Think of it.

> **Women must reject Machiavellian Mary as a leadership role model. In fact, we should not tolerate such Marys in our lives. We should out Machiavellian Mary and say, no more.**

If you are a successful entrepreneur, a real estate broker, a writer, a researcher, a lawyer, etc., and attend a conference where you see people who are at the beginning of their careers or have worked hard but not yet achieved success, what can you do to open a door? You may say, "I'll be inundated if I take that on." So what? In doing so, you may be the catalyst for many of these entrepreneurs, researchers, brokers, writers, etc. achieving their goals. And the reward for you will more than make-up for your time and effort.

If you are head of an academic department, how can you promote a junior faculty member? Do you have to be the first author on that publication? Aren't 200 publications enough for you? Shouldn't you share your wealth? How can you promote that person's achievements?

Whatever position you have, you do have the ability to do something for someone. Look for it. Do it.

Altruism. Is this focus on altruism merely nice talk? Really, who does it? Is anyone seriously interested in this other than some folks who appear in *Readers Digest* feel-good stories (we love these stories, by the way)? Well, Stanford University School of Medicine seemed to be interested, invested, and engaged in this. They developed a Center for Compassion Research and Education. They held "Compassion Cultivation" training and offered "Compassion Education." So, it's not just the stuff of fairytales.

The best food for psychological nourishment is altruism; giving to give, and not just to get. Paradoxically, giving boomerangs back on you with getting. This theme is certainly evident and inspiring, as in the life of Mother Teresa or Nelson Mandela. But in fact, there are many good and giving ordinary people all around us who can serve as inspirations. We've seen this in our lives. In big and small ways, doing for others has opened up opportunities that we had not anticipated. How many wonderful things are possible if women take this on and start the domino effect of splitting that creative atom in others?

Becoming hardened to others only hurts us. Both of us work in forensic mental health that has taken us into prisons, jails, and forensic mental hospitals. There are many people in these settings who have been accused or convicted of terrible crimes against others, and who themselves have been a victim, at some point in their lives, by others and/or by their mental illness. For some who work there, they may develop a spirit of impoverished thinking, of harshness, and lack of compassion because of the way they view these individuals. We wrote about in this in terms of a "toxic boomerang," where the stripping of empathy by becoming callused to the suffering of others in mental health forensic work can boomerang back onto the clinician who loses meaning in their work. This has the technical term of "compassion fatigue" but it goes beyond fatigue; it is something much more profound and toxic: a deadening of one's humanity. The cynical and hardened forensic clinician, correctional officer, or administrator has forgotten that all human interactions are bi-directional: what you do bounces right back onto you.

Inescapable network of mutuality

We are interconnected and interrelated: human connections that reverberate against one another. One psychologist, Albert Bandura, called this "reciprocal determinism" (the environment impacts us, but we also impact the environment).

Indeed, Dr. Martin Luther King said it best long ago, when he wrote about our "inescapable network of mutuality" while jailed for his role in non-violent protest of the injustices to African-Americans. This letter was crafted on April 16, 1963, in a Birmingham, Alabama jail on the margins of a newspaper, the only writing material he had. It was addressed to fellow clergymen, non-African-Americans, who criticized his activities as "outsiders coming in" to interfere with one town or

State's business. Dr. King replied, in essence, that when there is injustice there are no outsiders. Dr. King wrote, "I cannot sit idly by in Atlanta and not be concerned about what happens in Birmingham. Injustice anywhere is a threat to justice everywhere. We are caught in an inescapable network of mutuality, tied in a single garment of destiny. Whatever affects one directly, affects all indirectly." The violation of the rights of one set of human beings impacts not just that group, but everyone.

We are indeed tied in a "single garment of destiny" that we argue is the basis for why the cooperative spirit of helping others with fulfilling their dreams results in the larger gain of helping everyone. This inter-relatedness is also reflected in the Buddhist philosophy and the works of the Dalai Lama. The Dalai Lama has long advocated lovingkindness (see Daniel Goleman's book, *A Force for Good: The Dalai Lama's Vision for Our World)*, which in Christian spirituality is agape. In his book, Goleman writes of the Dalai Lama's vision of the force of good as a visible force, a movement that can, in essence, shift the tides of negativity through compassionate energy.

> **Let's start the feminine divine movement. Let's have it be a vibrant force, not invisible, but visible, and one that is strong and impactful. We are capable of this.**

Neuroscience also supports the type of entrepreneurial altruism that we are proposing. Matthieu Ricard, a Buddhist monk, writer, and scientist cites hundreds of neuroscience references, history, and religion to support this point: altruism is hardwired in the human brain and is linked to happiness.

This is what the feminine divine is all about. Imagine the joy that could be generated by releasing the feminine divine creative atom splitters! Why isn't this view prominent in our thinking? The female spiritual core has, no doubt, taken a second place status throughout the ages; maybe some even question whether enlightenment can be achieved in the female form. But WE still retain that unique ability to give birth to children, and to be mothers.

Mothering is a spiritual practice: it is nurturing, loving, and other-oriented. Mothering is a core aspect of the feminine divine, whether you have ever borne a child or not. Women can "mother" in many ways: including nurturing and developing the destiny of others. In doing so, we too will benefit.

Think of how many ideas die, or are never sown. What have we lost in the realm of creative potential? What have we lost in books, poems, artwork? In inventions? In products?

Women have the potential to change that. We don't have to be snared by competition, or driven by the fear that if we give we will lose our edge. That's not our nature anyway. We are inclined toward cooperation.

Always ask yourself this, "What can I do to unleash a dream in others?" Whatever your role– you may not be a CEO or a department head, but you do have a sphere of control. Use it.

Let's start the feminine divine movement

Let's have it be a vibrant force, not invisible, but visible, and one that is strong and impactful. We are capable of this. Let's make it so that all women are discovering how we can be a creative atom splitter. We can start this and carry it through, and soon it will unleash a tsunami of potential.

Isn't cooperation and sharing a much better way to live than hoarding success? Isn't this better than being the handmaiden to Machiavellian Mary? Women nurturing our feminine divine spirit can become an incredible force that begins a domino effect of a change in business, in politics, in academia, in science and technology, and in the artistic endeavors. We can do this. We can be net-doers who use what we have to bring to reality the dreams of others.

That is the ultimate psychological nourishment: of living life with an emotional pyramid firmly set on the ground of self-actualization, and of atom splitting the creativity of others.

That's the incredible power of the Feminine Divine.

FOOD FOR THOUGHT

Bstan-'Dzin-Rgya-Mtsho, D. L. (2008). *The Dalai Lama: Essential writings.* T. A. Forsthoefel (Ed.), Maryknoll, NY: Orbis Books.

Brown, B. (2009). *Living beauty.* Boston & NY: Springboard Press.

Brown, B. (2012). *Pretty powerful.* San Francisco: Chronicle Books.

Eastwood, J. D., Frischen, A., Fenske, M. J., & Smilek, D. (2012). The unengaged mind: Defining boredom in terms of attention. *Perspectives on Psychological Science. 7(5):* 482-495. doi: 10.1177/1745691612456044

Edwards, J. (1741). Sinners in the Hands of an Angry God. A Sermon Preached at Enfield, July 8th, 1741. R. Smolinski, Reiner, (Ed.) *Electronic Texts in American Studies.* Paper 54. http://digitalcommons. unl.edu/cgi/viewcontent.cgi?article=1053&context=etas

Fienup-Riordan, A. (2005). *Wise words of the Yup'ik people.* Lincoln & London: University of Nebraska Press.

Frankl, V. E. (1969). *The will to meaning: Foundations and applications of Logotherapy.* New York, NY: World Publishing Company.

Frankl, V. E. (1984). *Man's search for meaning.* New York: Washington Square Press.

Goebel, B. L., & Brown, D. R. (1981). Age differences in motivation related to Maslow's need hierarchy. *Developmental Psychology,* 17(6), 809–815. doi:10.1037/0012-1649.17.6.809

Hannum, R. D., Rosellini, R. A. & Seligman, M. E. (1976). Learned helplessness in the rat: Retention and immunization. *Developmental Psychology, 12(5),* 449-454.

Hardin, C. D, & Higgins, E. T. (1996). Shared reality: How social verification makes the subjective objective. In R. M. Sorrentino & E. T. Higgins (Eds.), *Handbook of motivation and cognition (*3rd ed.). (28–84). New York, NY: Guilford.

Jung, C. G. (1971) *Psychological types: Collected works of C. G. Jung,* Volume 6. (H. G. Baynes, Trans., Revision by R. F. C. Hull). Princeton, NJ: Princeton University Press.

Jung, C. G. ([1961] 1989). *Memories, dreams, reflections.* (R. Winston & C. Winston, Trans.). New York, NY: Vantage Books

Kafka, F. ([1915]2009) *The metamorphosis.* (D. Wyllie, Trans.). Classix Press.

Kenrick, D. T.; Griskevicius, V.; Neuberg, S. L.; & Schaller, M. (2010). Renovating the pyramid of needs: Contemporary extensions built upon ancient foundations. *Perspectives on Psychological Science, 5(3),* 292-314. Doi:10.1177/1745691610369469

King, M.L. (April 16, 1963) Letter from a Birmingham Jail [King, Jr.]. Birmingham, Alabama. Accessed through University of Pennsylvania African Studies Center, http://www.africa.upenn.edu/Articles_Gen/Letter_Birmingham.html

Lewis, C. S. (1942). *The Screwtape letters.* London: Geoffrey Bles.

Markides, K. C. (2008). Eastern Orthodox mysticism and transpersonal theory. *Journal of Transpersonal Psychology, 40(2),* 178–198.

Maslow, A.H. (1943). A theory of human motivation. *Psychological Review, 50(4),* 370–396.

Maslow, A. (1954). *Motivation and personality.* New York, NY: Harper.

Miller, W. R., & Seligman, M. E. (1975). Depression and learned helplessness in man. *Journal of Abnormal Psychology, 84(3),* 228-238.

Rutters, F. Pilz, S., Koopman, A. D. M., Rauth, S. P., Power, F., Stehouwer, C. D. A.,...Dekker, J. M. (2015). Stressful life events and incident of metabolic syndrome: the Hoorn study. *Stress: The International Journal on the Biology of Stress,* online publication date July 17, 2015, doi: 10.3109/10253890.2015.1064891

Smee, D., Sreenivasan, S., & Weinberger, L. E. (2009). *Totally American: Harnessing the dynamic duo of optimism and resilience to achieve success.* Los Angeles: HolyMoly Press.

Seligman, M. E. P., Steen, T. A., Park, N., & Peterson, C. (2005). Positive psychology progress: Empirical validation of interventions. *American Psychologist, 60(10),* 410–421.

Tolstoy, L. (2003. *Walk in the Light (and Twenty-Three Tales)* Maryknoll, NY: Orbis Books.

Tugade, M. M. & Fredrickson, B. L.(2004). Resilient individuals use positive emotions to bounce back from negative emotional experiences. *Journal of Personality and Social Psychology, 86(2),* 320–333.

Wilder, T. (1954). *The matchmaker.* New York: Samuel French.

ACKNOWLEDGEMENTS

Special thanks to Deirdre Devlin, LCSW for her review of portions of this work.

Special thanks to Etan Markowitz, Ph.D. for review of references and material related to physics and science.

Special thanks to Bob Newlon for consultation and conceptual formulation of the cover.

Special thanks to Daniel E. Smee, M.S.W. for contributions to the chapters on psychological staleness and hoarding.

ABOUT THE AUTHORS

Shoba Sreenivasan earned a Ph.D. in Clinical Psychology from UCLA in 1986 and thereafter completed a forensic post-doctoral fellowship at USC. She is a Clinical Professor at Keck School of Medicine of USC, works as a VA psychologist, and has a private forensic psychology practice. She has co-authored *Totally American*, a motivational book, and authored the *Mattie Spyglass* series. She has also written numerous scholarly publications and book chapters in the fields of forensic psychology, violence risk assessment, and Veterans' issues.

Linda E. Weinberger earned a Ph.D. in Clinical Psychology from the University of Houston in 1979 and subsequently completed a postdoctoral forensic fellowship at USC. She has been the Chief Psychologist at the USC Institute of Psychiatry, Law, and Behavioral Sciences, and Professor of Clinical Psychiatry at Keck School of Medicine of USC for over three and a half decades. She is the author of numerous book chapters and scholarly publications in the fields of forensic psychology, suicide risk, and violence risk assessment.

30169640R00099

Made in the USA
Middletown, DE
15 March 2016